The One Belt One Road (OBOR) Initiative and the Port of Piraeus

The One Belt One Road (OBOR) Initiative and the Port of Piraeus

Understanding Greece's Role in China's Strategy to Construct a Unified Large Market

By Tatiana Gontika

Routledge
Taylor & Francis Group

NEW YORK AND LONDON

First published 2022
by Routledge
600 Broken Sound Parkway #300, Boca Raton FL, 33487

and by Routledge
2 Park Square, Milton Park, Abingdon, Oxon, OX14 4RN

Routledge is an imprint of the Taylor & Francis Group, an informa business

ISBN: 978-1-032-05151-2 (hbk)
ISBN: 978-1-032-05152-9 (pbk)
ISBN: 978-1-003-19631-0 (ebk)

Typeset in Minion
by Apex CoVantage, LLC

This book is dedicated to my family and people who were close to me and encouraged me to take up this challenge.

Contents

Preface

June 2016 Athens, Greece: The members of the Hellenic Parliament ratify a deal between COSCO and the Piraeus Port Authority. In the midst of Greece's severe socioeconomic crisis, Chinese company COSCO offered €280.5 million in return to 51% of the Piraeus Port.

Why did China commit to what is estimated to be an €800 million investment plan in defaulted Greece? What is the Belt and Road Initiative? Which countries are included and which not? Who will benefit and who are more skeptical about it? It all started after the first assignment during the first week of the first semester of my master's degree program. As the research went on, I realized that the present became past as the Belt and Road Initiative intertwined with the ancient Silk Road showing the way to the future.

To answer my questions, a detailed analysis and comparison of the Silk Road and the Belt and Road Initiative were necessary. Moreover, as the main focus of the book is China and Greece, the reader will be introduced to their history, focusing on various key events, and a detailed examination of their shipping industries over the years.

What differentiates the book from others is the combination of primary and secondary research. At a very early stage of my investigation, I felt the need to contact individuals from different fields, backgrounds, and cultures and interview them. Their opinions are presented and discussed throughout the book, thus embracing different perspectives on the topic.

In conclusion, the book focuses on what appears to be one of the most successful investments included in the Belt and Road Initiative, benefiting both countries.

Acknowledgments

I would like to express my gratitude to my professor and supervisor, Dr. Lawrence A. Howard; without his guidance and support, I would not have been able to complete this thesis. I would also like to thank the people who made time to answer my questions and contribute in their own way to my project.

About the Author

Tatiana Gontika was born in Athens, Greece, on September 8, 1992, where she spent the first 18 years of her life. In 2010, she was accepted in Goldsmiths College, University of London, where she received a BA in Anthropology. After graduating, she moved to Medellin, Colombia, where she volunteered in a leading institution in promoting human rights and protecting public interest. A few months later she moved to Buenos Aires, Argentina, where she made a career change and went into the shipping industry. After four years, she was ready for the next chapter in her life and decided to apply to SUNY Maritime College, from which she graduated in 2020 with an MSc in International Transportation Management. Having lived ten years abroad, she has decided to move back to home and pursue her life's dreams in Athens.

Chapter 1

Introduction

One Belt One Road (OBOR), a signature initiative of Chinese President Xi Jinping, seems to be one of the most frequently discussed enterprises in the world today. This controversial mix of worldwide projects has put China and Xi in the center of attention and not always in a positive way. Of course, not all projects included in the initiative have been or are likely to be successful, but the initiative has far-ranging economic, cultural, and political potential.

OBOR, in its essence, is an attempt of the Chinese government to secure for the country a paramount position in global finance and ensure that primacy extends far into the future. In particular, it is an attempt to ensure enough natural resources to support China in the long term. Therefore, the areas picked for the implementation and development of OBOR are deliberately strategic. One of the countries in which China has picked to invest, and which is a main focus of this thesis, is Greece, specifically the port of Piraeus.

It is naïve to think that such a project is a new concept. The OBOR initiative has many similarities to the ancient *Silk Road*. Although the ancient route and modern concept are in no way identical, when the two are compared many similarities rise. The main difference between the two is that the Silk Road was created somewhat organically, whereas the OBOR is planned in detail. On the other hand, the main similarity is the fact that both represent a network of trade. Moreover, both combine land and sea transport.

To understand China's motivation to build such a network, an examination of some of its history is in order.

This thesis divides a historical overview of China into three main eras: (1) Emperor rule, (2) the transition from emperors to governors, and (3) the modern Chinese Republic. During the first two phases, China was a major player in the Silk Road, and during the third one, China is the mastermind behind the OBOR.

While examining China's history, it is important to keep in mind the four industrial revolutions,[1] because China did not follow the rest of the world and compressed all four stages in under fifty years.[2] The First Industrial Revolution took place during the second half of the 18th century and transformed the primarily agricultural societies into industrial. The Second Industrial Revolution lasted from the late 19th century until the early 20th century and was also focused mainly on industrialization and mass production of consumer goods. The Third Industrial Revolution is the digital revolution that has been occurring since the middle of the last century. In 1954, for example, General Electric installed the UNIVAVAC I computer. A year later, in 1955, John Hancock Mutual Life Insurance Co. digitalized their customer information.[3] These are only two of the numerous examples of companies who transitioned using digital administrative and/or operational systems. Finally, the Fourth Industrial Revolution, though sometimes perceived as a continuation of the third, is still digital but defers in the velocity, scope, and systems impact.[4] A milestone event of the Fourth Industrial Revolution is the opening of the Internet to all users. An initiative established and seen through by the George H.W. Bush administration.[5]

China's position today is only in part due to its political and socioeconomic past. A big part of China is its maritime industry and the companies associated with it. Analytically, it is useful to divide an overview of Chinese shipping into two periods. The first one covers the establishment of the People's Republic of China in 1949 until the death of Mao Tse Tung in 1976 and the primacy of Deng Xiao Ping in 1978. The second period is from 1978 to date. The first period happened under a period of planned economy in China, whereas the second continues to take place in a more open economy. This division is analytically useful because the first phase of Chinese shipping is the initial development and it was greatly based on leasing foreign vessels. During the second phase, China established its own merchant fleet and became a major player in international shipping and ship building.

Chinese shipping is closely connected to some shipping companies, which have transformed along the way. This thesis focuses in depth on *China Ocean Shipping Company* (COSCO), because it is the one involved in the port of Piraeus. COSCO, although allegedly an independent entity, is very much associated with and is a direct extension of the Chinese government.

A deep understanding of China's maritime history is founded on an understanding of the importance of both ancient and modern trading networks. Through the study of the ancient Silk Road network, one can comprehend how surprisingly connected the world was back then. Goods produced in the far east found their way to Greece and Rome and vice versa. Of course, the routes were affected by political change or social instability, and therefore, new trading points were sometimes created. One of the most well-known travelers of the Silk Road was Marco Polo, who along with his family completed a 24-year round trip from Rome to China and traveled most of the Silk Road routes. Marco Polo was the only one to document and publish detailed analysis and description of his travels through which important information is preserved.

Transitioning from the ancient Silk Road to the OBOR initiative has been neither easy nor smooth, but it is reality. The initiative includes over one-third of the countries in the world in one way or another.[6] Various trade agreements have been signed affecting, or are a result of, the diplomatic relations of the signees. Additionally, due to the financial crisis of 2008 and the more recent refugee crisis, countries around the world, and especially in Europe, are experiencing political changes.

These events, as well as other factors, are crucial context of the establishment of OBOR. Trading is versatile and constantly changing, thus alternative networks must always be considered. Bearing that in mind, the possible routes and their political and financial consequences need assessment, both by Chinese planners, and by those who wish to study OBOR from afar.

OBOR has three alternative routes: the maritime, the south land, and the north land. Each of them includes different countries and of course, contains its own advantages and disadvantages. One of the countries that is a candidate for inclusion in more than one of the routes due to its geographical location is Greece.

Greece, similar to China, has a long line of history. However, for the purpose of this thesis only certain threads of its modern, post-Ottoman history are discussed in detail. An overview of its political and financial instabilities is crucial in order to comprehend the country's recent financial and social crisis. Greece's modern identity is an outcome of a very bloody civil war, a dictatorship, and very bad fund management. Social phenomena, such as the brain drain, are Greece's contemporary reality because of the lack of opportunities for the new generation and the struggling of the older one. At the same time, high taxation and various other policies have discouraged foreign investments.

One of the Greek industries that have always been strong and mostly dependent on international resources has been the shipping industry. Thus, the port of Piraeus has historically been a center for trading and tourism. It is not a coincidence that Piraeus port is such a big part of the OBOR initiative. Having been destroyed and rebuilt various times, it has managed to become one of the busiest and most efficient European ports. Its historical importance and geopolitical significance would likely be less if Greece had not traditionally been a shipping country.

Greeks have been in the center of the maritime industry since the early 1820s and remain in that role today. Over the years, Greek maritime centers have shifted, but the Chiot and the Ionian families have always been key to the evolution of the industry. Greek shipowners realized that vessels are assets and thus traded them as they saw appropriate and had no emotional attachment. Moreover, due to WWI and WWII, the shipping industry experienced major changes and reshuffling. Finally, the Greek state in its recent history has tried to attract and benefit shipowners. Although many are based in Piraeus, they still remain independent from the country's domestic financial reality.

However, they are not able, especially if their vessels operate in Greece, to remain independent to Piraeus port and its change of management. The change of any administration creates obstacles to continued smooth operation, but the involvement of a foreign entity creates additional uncertainty and a fear of the unknown. Fortunately, the privatization of the Piraeus port was somewhat smooth and definitely necessary.

This project, of course, did not happen overnight. Various discussions took place on an international level and domestically until all parties came to an agreement. The deal and change at Piraeus between Greece and China affect more than the politicians and the shipowners, and it affects everyone involved in the port's operations as well as the residents of the area. To further comprehend the impact on their lives, one must see things through their eyes, and there is no better way than contacting individuals and conversing with them.

Finally, as do all changes or development projects, both the Piraeus port and the OBOR initiative have consequences on domestic and international levels. Such consequences affect both port and initiative in financial and environmental aspects, of which neither can be ignored. In conclusion, the specific deal at Piraeus and the OBOR initiative as a whole have the potential of benefiting the international and local communities. However, specific measures must be taken and governments must collaborate in order for the deal in Piraeus and the OBOR initiative to have the most beneficial and the least negative impact.

NOTES

1 The idea of a "Fourth Industrial Revolution" is currently being used and may or may not remain accurate in the future. The first time the term "fourth industrial revolution" was used was in 2015 in an article written by Klaus Schwab, the executive chairman of the World Economic Forum.

2 Wen, Yi. "China's Rise from Agrarian Society to Industrial Power | St. Louis Fed." *Federal Reserve Bank of St. Louis | Economic Data, Monetary Rates, Economic Education.* Last modified April 12, 2016. www.stlouisfed.org/publications/regional-economist/april-2016/chinas-rapid-rise-from-backward-agrarian-society-to-industrial-powerhouse-in-just-35-years.

3 Press, Gil. "A Very Short History of Digitization." *Forbes.* Last modified January 11, 2016. www.forbes.com/sites/gilpress/2015/12/27/a-very-short-history-of-digitization/#7e1a148649ac.

4 Schwab, Klaus. "The Fourth Industrial Revolution: What It Means and How to Respond." *World Economic Forum.* Last modified November 21, 2019. www.weforum.org/agenda/2016/01/the-fourth-industrial-revolution-what-it-means-and-how-to-respond/.

5 "Bush Calls for Universal Broadband by 2007." *Msnbc.com.* Last modified March 26, 2004. www.nbcnews.com/id/4609864/ns/technology_and_science-tech_and_gadgets/t/bush-calls-universal-broadband/#.XdLsyDJKi_s.

6 Afghanistan, Albania, Armenia, Austria, Azerbaijan, Bangladesh, Belarus, Bosnia and Herzegovina, Brunei, Cambodia, Chile, Croatia, Cyprus, Czech Republic, Djibouti, Egypt, Estonia, Ethiopia, Georgia, Greece, Hungary, Indonesia, Italy, Kazakhstan, Kenya, Kyrgyzstan, Latvia, Laos, Lithuania, Malaysia, Mongolia, Moldova, Mozambique, Myanmar, Nepal, Oman, Pakistan, Papua, New Guinea, The Philippines, Poland, Portugal, Russia, Saudi Arabia, Serbia, Singapore, Sri Lanka, Switzerland, Tajikistan, Thailand, The United Arab Emirates, Turkey, Ukraine, Uzbekistan, Vietnam. Other South American, Caribbean, European, and African countries are also involved but not as much as the aforementioned countries.

Chapter 2

China's Historical Overview

China is the world's third largest country in area and has the largest population in the world. Politically and economically, China today is a result of cumulative regime changes. Some regimes expanded the country's borders and external influence. On the other hand, weak regimes decreased China's geopolitical power and caused domestic division. This pattern of expansion and contraction is readily evident from the historical record, beginning with China's first known dynasty and continuing through to today. Based on this record, this thesis divides Chinese history into three eras as follows: (1) emperor rule; (2) the transition from emperors to governors; and (3) modern China as a Republic.

The Shang Dynasty established the first known, organized, Chinese state. According to Liu Xin's calculations, the Shang Dynasty ruled from 1766 BC to 1122 BC.[1] However, according to the Bamboo Annals,[2] the Shang Dynasty was in power from 1556 BC to 1046 BC. The Shang Dynasty is believed to have united a large part of North-Central China. It is believed that the last Shang King committed suicide after his defeat by Wu of Zhou. The Zhou Dynasty lasted almost 800 years, making it the longest lasting dynasty in Chinese history. The Zhou Dynasty period is divided into two sections. The first ranges from 1045 BC to 770 BC, during which the Dynasty initially prevailed in Northern China and then occupied and united large parts of the country. The second ranges from 770 BC to 256 BC, known as the Eastern Zhou. During this second period, the Dynasty's political power collapsed and the authority became decentralized as many villages and towns developed their own local rulers. The inability of the Zhou monarchs to unite their kingdom led to instability and wars between the various, self-proclaimed, independent states.

Over three decades passed until the country was able to reunite and reestablish itself. King Ying Zheng of Qin restored domestic peace in 221 BC.

King Ying Zheng, the first Qin Emperor (Qin Shihuangdi), became the first ruler to use the title "emperor." The Qin rule lasted only 15 years, and the empire collapsed after Ying Zheng's death. Despite the short period of the dynasty, it is one of the most culturally significant. Even though the Great Wall of China can be traced back well before the Qin Dynasty, it was under Ying Zheng that existing walls between the states were unified. Thus, conceiving the idea of the wall as we know it today. The Han Dynasty started in 206 BC, a significant milestone because the Han years, 206 BC to AD 220, are defined by BBC's article *China's profile—Timeline*[3] as the first Chinese "golden age."

The most important characteristic of the period was the ability of the emperors to govern China as a whole. Economic and cultural growth flourished because of the geographic unity that the Han emperors created. However, in the years following the collapse of the Han Dynasty, the very opposite occurred. The country was divided; aspiring emperors and their desire to govern led to many wars. This period of unrest ended in AD 581 with the rise of the Sui Dynasty. The first Sui emperor reunited and started redeveloping China.

The following almost 300-year Tang Dynasty consists of some of the most significant high points of Chinese civilization. During the Tang rule, China's influence reached into Central Asia for the first time. Thereafter, in 960, the Song Dynasty followed into power and lasted until 1279. It was during the Song period that both literature and scientific innovation blossomed, simultaneously with enormous commercial growth.

Subsequently, the Mongols defeated the Song and established the Yuan Dynasty. The Yuan Dynasty was founded by Kublai Khan and lasted from 1279 to 1368. The most significant event during the Yuan rule was the decision to make Beijing the capital of China. Moreover, individuals from Europe and Western Asia, including Marco Polo, reached China. In 1368, the Mongol Yuan Dynasty was overthrown and the Ming Dynasty came to power. It was during this time that China benefitted from its strength as a military power, creating a centralized, bureaucratic system and establishing a strong agricultural economy.

The Great Wall of China was completed during the culturally significant Ming years and took the form it has now. Moreover, the Ming sponsored a range of sea voyages under Admiral Zheng He, whose fleets sailed the Indian Ocean as far as the Persian Gulf and eastern coast of Africa.

The Ming Dynasty was in power for almost 300 years, but it was not until the Manchu Qing Dynasty that China reached its zenith. The Qing

Dynasty is the last imperial dynasty of China and was in power from 1644 to 1911. During these years, the empire's territory grew significantly. Moreover, the population grew from approximately 150 million to 450 million during the Ming Dynasty. The population of the Chinese empire then consisted of non-Chinese minorities, which were sinicized. Additionally, it was under the Qing rule that China had a unified national economy, characterized by common interests and goals.

The 19th century is characterized by the falling of the Qing Dynasty. During this time, the Western powers imposed "unequal treaties" that created foreign concessions in China's ports. The dynasty's decline along with the crisis in China's ports led to sociopolitical instability. Regional warlords took power, making it impossible for the central government to rule. The peak of China's decay took place during the "Boxer Rebellion." The Qing administration attempted to exile foreigners from Northern China, but its mission was unsuccessful. Western powers allied with Russia and Japan defeated the administration, further weakening the Qing government.

In 1912, after a long period of hostilities and instability, the country became a republic. This, however, did not appreciably improve the situation, and the people of China continued experiencing both political and military instability. Aiming to change this and with personal aspirations to power, Sun Yat-sen and Liao Chonzhen founded the Chinese Nationalist Party, Kuomintang of China. At the same time, Mao Zedong, Zhou Enlai, Chen Duxiu, and Li Dazhao founded the Communist Party of China serving as opposition. Although fundamentally opposed in ideology, the two parties cooperated during the second Sino-Japanese War. Shortly after the defeat of Japan in 1945, a three-year civil war broke out leading to the death of over 12 million people. In October 1949, the Communist Party led by Mao Zedong won, establishing the People's Republic of China.

The first years after the establishment of the people's republic were not prosperous. Mass starvation, malnutrition, and diseases were part of the Chinese reality. The government divided the country into 50,000 communes and each of them was dedicated to excel in farming or industry or education. A year after the country's establishment, in 1950, the Agrarian Reform Law was passed, according to which the land of landlords and wealthy farmers were redistributed. A few years later, Rural Collectivization began, wherein individual landownership was eradicated and replaced with "cooperatives." Moreover, during the same decade, goods and food were rationed in households and the income gap between rural and urban populations grew even more.

Chairman Mao commenced the "Great Leap Forward" initiative in an attempt to further push the country's industrialization. The five-year initiative, however failed, was abandoned two years later, and the people of China saw history repeat itself. Famine and disease began to spread throughout the country again. In what was arguably one of the largest famines in human history, lasting from 1959 through 1961. Four years later, under Chairman Mao, local authorities were put on trial and historic customs were questioned in an attempt to give the Communist Party more power. Through the Great Proletarian Cultural Revolution, Mao revived a revolutionary spirit and created major social, economic, and political disturbance.

After Mao's death in 1976, Deng Xiaoping became China's leader. It was under his regime that the country experienced economic liberalization combined with a kind of government-controlled capitalism. During this change, the government remained strong and China reached economic and political stability.

In 1978, Deng Xiaoping started his Four Modernization program in an attempt to reset the country's goals. The four sectors consisted of agriculture, industrial science, technology, and national defense. In order to modernize agriculture, Deng introduced mechanization combined with what he called the responsibility system. The system was a way to make sure that all farmers were involved and each family could produce more than they needed. If a family was unable to produce due to a lack of land, the government leased land to them and they had to repay by selling, at a set price, part of their harvest. The remainder of their crops was sold in an open market for profit.

The second sector was the nation's industry. During Mao's era, the country focused on developing mining and military weapons. Moreover, their focus was quantity over quality in products like furniture, tools, and so on. Deng, however, emphasized light industry, such as consumer goods. He extended the responsibility system to this sector too, allowing managers to profit on a personal level.

The third, and arguably most important, aspect of Deng's project was removing China's policy of isolation. His aim was for China to attract ideas of technology and trade and to do so he established the "Open-door Policy." Through it, Deng attracted and encouraged outside investors to develop the private economic sector. To further enhance this trend, he created the first Special Economic Zones (SEZ) in southeastern China. According to his plan, local governments of the designated areas were able to offer tax incentives to any foreign investor without the approval of the central government.

The fourth, and final, sector was China's defense forces. The country's military weapons were outdated. Deng, therefore, focused on both researching and manufacturing new, up-to-date weaponry. However, he encouraged the use of both the new and pre-existing weapons. Additionally, he modernized the training of the soldiers and increased the size of the military.

Along with the Four Modernization program, the Xiaoping government made a series of reforms leading to less government-controlled businesses. Moreover, during the 1980s, many of the state enterprises were privatized, contributing to China's economic growth. China launched its largest SEZ in 1990. Located in the outskirts of Shanghai, it was intended to transform the area into the country's new financial and commercial hub. In addition to the SEZ, in 1990, the Shanghai Stock Market re-opened for the first time since 1949 (see Figure 2.1).[4] From this moment, as shown in the graph, China's economy went through substantial growth.

The 2000s mark an important decade for both Chinese international relations and international trade. In 2001, 52 years after the establishment of the People's Republic of China, the country was admitted to the World

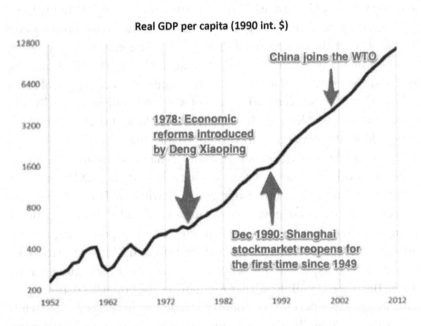

FIGURE 2.1
China's Economic Growth (1952–2012).

Trade Organization. In 2003, China and India reached an agreement regarding cross-border trading. Only a year later, China signed a landmark multilateral trade agreement. The agreement was signed by ten more Southeast Asian countries and aimed to unite 25% of the world's population in a free-trade zone.[5] In 2006, a new railway, the Qinghai–Tibet line started operating, becoming the world's highest altitude train route.

Only a few months later, in November 2006, leaders from various African states assembled in Beijing.[6] According to the official website of China's Ministry of Foreign Affairs, China and the various African states agreed on sociopolitical, economic cooperation, and international affairs cooperation.[7] During the summit, special attention was drawn to economic cooperation. More specifically, the Chinese government committed to supporting Chinese banks that were to set up by the *China–Africa Development Fund*, which is estimated to gradually reach $5 billion.[8] During President Hu Jintao's visit to several African states, various human rights groups accused the Chinese government of dealing with corrupt and/or abusive regimes.

Simultaneous to China's African outreach, Japan and China negotiated on developing a gas field in the East China Sea. The Chunxiao field, due to its geographical location, had always been an issue of dispute between the two countries. On August 5, 2006, *China National Offshore Oil Corp* (CNOO) announced that the gas field was under full-scale production.[9] The dispute over the ownership of the economic interests of the area were, of course, further inflamed after this statement. The high tensions over the East China Sea kept escalating with both countries ordering patrol ships to shadow each other, generating fear of a greater outburst. Finally, the two countries were able to reach an agreement in June 2008,[10] under which they would jointly develop hydrocarbons in the area.

The year 2008 was a significant year for China in addition to the aforementioned deal with Japan because China hosted the XXIX Summer Olympics. In November of the same year, following the Lehman Brothers bankruptcy, the Chinese government announced a $585 billion stimulus packages.[11] Their goal was to stimulate the economy, preventing it from slowing down. The global financial crisis had affected China more than the government had expected. While most countries were struggling, China became the largest trading partner for many of the powerful nations.

During the same period, the country's trade surplus exceeded $250 billion.[12] In early 2009, Russia and China came to a $25 billion agreement, under which Russia would provide China with oil for the next two decades

in exchange for loans.[13] Despite the negative effect that the global financial crisis had on the Chinese economy, in 2010, China posted a 17.7%
rise in exports in December. This made China the world's largest exporter
followed by Germany. A year later, however, China overtook Japan and
became the world's second largest economy.[14]

Political scandals, change of government, and a slowdown of the economy
characterized the following years. Xi Jinping was named Vice Chairman
in 2010 and became the leader of the Communist Party in 2012. A few
months later, in March 2013, he became president. During his first years
as the country's leader, China fell from being the world's largest economy
to being the second largest. In February 2014, the country's trade surplus
went up 14% compared to that of 2013,[15] enhancing concerns regarding
China's economic slowdown. Concerns were confirmed a year later when
China's economic growth fell to its lowest for over 20 years, leading the
government to revise growth targets. The *International Monetary Fund*
(IMF) forecasted further deterioration in the upcoming years, extrapolat-
ing from the continuously declining trend of 2016.[16]

In October 2017, re-elected General Secretary of the Central Committee
of the Communist Party, Xi Jinping, held the 19th National Congress of
the Communist Party of China. While addressing the press, Xi Jinping
committed to fulfill and hopefully surpass the five-year plan he and his
team had put together. Part of the plan was to continue establishing China
as an important international force, following the trend of the previous
decades. The General Secretary prioritized the transformation of society
through innovation. Additionally, he reassured that the Party's pledge to
transform China's growth model had not changed, indicating that the
consumption and services-driven model will be supported through various initiatives and is a key for the future of the Chinese economy.

One of the major issues discussed was China's role in the Fourth
Industrial Revolution. The government's goal has been to transform China
from being a follower to being a leader[17] by successfully implementing sup-
portive policies. Moreover, the Party encouraged both public and private
investments, and finally, large companies were to make their resources
available to smaller companies. The government gave additional support
for small, growing firms. Through these policies, it domestically supported
entrepreneurship and technological innovation and will continue to affect
the way in which observers perceive the country.

Another major issue was international trade and its promotion. General
Secretary Xi acknowledged China's financial dependence on the global

economy. In 2017, many developed countries adopted protectionist policies, affecting not only China but other emerging market economies too.

One of the most representative strategies on cross-border trade from the Chinese perspective is the OBOR initiative. Through it, the Chinese government is expecting to play an active role in international trade, capital, and information flow. Such projects are seen by the Chinese as a way to reignite globalization. This, however, should not be taken as a sign that the Chinese government focuses on the economic greater good but rather to China's greater good. In cases where globalization does not assist the government's goals toward a successful initiative, they should not be expected to follow.

International trade has been a focal point of China's international politics and a driving factor of its economy during the past decades. One of the ways the government has succeeded in opening up the economy and promoting China as a trading partner is by signing *Free Trade Agreements* (FTAs). FTAs are signed by at least two nations and through them the participants agree on the terms of trade.[18] By signing an FTA, the members agree to freely trade, thus eliminating trade barriers between them but maintain those against third parties. FTAs, as stated in the official website of the *Ministry of Commerce of the People's Republic of China*, are viewed as a platform to effectively integrate into global economy and strengthen economic cooperation with other economies. Currently, China is part of 20 such agreements and is negotiating 12 more.[19]

Although China is an economic superpower in today's world, the nation does not participate in all the mega-regional trade agreements (MRTAs) of the Asia–Pacific Region. Being the center of the continuing changes of the trade world, the Asia–Pacific Region is also the center of three of the largest MRTAs. Two of them are currently negotiated, one among China–Japan–South Korea and a second one known as the Regional Comprehensive Economic Partnership, amongst Pacific Rim countries and not including any country of the Americas. The only active MRTA of the region is the Trans-Pacific Partnership (TPP), currently signed by 11 countries. The aim of the agreement was to provide free trade for the Pacific Rim countries; it included the United States who withdrew in 2017 and excluded China.

The TPP was seen by the Obama administration as a socio-political tool to institutionalize a "super-sized" next-generation trade deal, including free movement of not only goods and services but also capital and labor.[20] Moreover, the TPP agenda was disconnected with the regional initiatives and terms on exports and imports were made largely by the United States. It was because of these characteristics that the agreement was viewed by the Obama Administration as a strategic medium of the United States to influence the region and undermine China's role in Asia's economy. The agreement aimed to force China to reconsider its regional relationships as an economic superpower and its trade with member countries of the TPP as well as its overall welfare would suffer irrespective of the United States' participation.

During his pre-electoral campaign, President Trump had referred to the TPP as a "horrible deal" various times.[21] His main argument for this was the fact that through this deal many Americans would lose their jobs. This argument is not entirely wrong because, most probably, the United States would have outsourced to developing countries. Fewer labor laws as well as an overall lower cost of labor would indeed attract many companies who would want to minimize their expenses. Moreover, during her campaign Hillary Clinton, who had originally supported the deal, stated in an interview with PBS that she would not support it.[22] Upon his election, President Trump did indeed withdraw from the TPP agreement. The United States' withdrawal from the TPP did not appear to significantly affect the historically hostile relations between the United States and China.

Since 2018, the United States has imposed high tariffs and negotiations between the two countries have proven difficult. Earlier this year, the IMF lowered its 2019 growth forecast for China.[23] The trade war between the two countries is obviously affecting both, and the governments have been preparing for additional tariffs. In an attempt to mutually benefit, the two countries are currently negotiating a new trade agreement. The "Phase 1" agreement has been negotiated since early October 2018 and though it was supposed to be signed by November it appears it will be postponed until December 2019.[24]

The "Phase 1" agreement comes at a time where both sides need a "win." On the one hand, with President Trump's reelection campaign currently underway a new, beneficial, agreement can reinforce his position. On the other hand, the agreement represents some kind of trade stability for President Xi, whose country is currently experiencing a relatively low annual rate growth.[25]

If the agreement goes through, it will include up to $50 billion[26] worth of American agricultural products bought by China. Additionally, the proposed deal will strengthen Chinese protections for American intellectual property as well as trademark issues.[27] Another term of the agreement will be the financial services and access for American firms into the Chinese market. For China, the benefit of this agreement will be more imminent, as the United States will not impose the December 15 tariffs.[28] Large part of the negotiations is focused on tariffs as the Chinese side aims to remove most, is not all, tariffs imposed by the United States.

Even though the Chinese economy overall is going through one of its roughest phases, one sector has not been so severely hit; the maritime industry remains one of the country's driving forces. Constantly evolving and involved in new projects, China has established its position in the center of the global shipping scene.

NOTES

1   Liu Xin (50 BC–23 BC), also known as Liu Xiu, was a Chinese astronomer, mathematician, historian, librarian, and politician.
2   Bamboo Annals is a set of Chinese court records and contains one of the few written records of the earliest period in Chinese history.
3   "China Profile." *BBC News*. Last modified July 29, 2019. www.bbc.com/news/world-asia-pacific-13017882.
4   Illustration from: "A Brief History of China's Economic Growth." *World Economic Forum*. Last modified December 4, 2019. www.weforum.org/agenda/2015/07/brief-history-of-china-economic-growth/.
5   "China Profile." *BBC News*. Last modified July 29, 2019. www.bbc.com/news/world-asia-pacific-13017882.
6   African countries participating in this assembly will be hereon considered as *one* and China will be hereon considered *one*.
7   "Forum on China-Africa Cooperation Beijing Action Plan (2007–2009)." 欢迎访问中华人民共和国外交部网站. Last modified November 5, 2019. www.fmprc.gov.cn/zflt/eng/zyzl/hywj/t280369.htm.
8   "Forum on China-Africa Cooperation Beijing Action Plan (2007–2009)." 欢迎访问中华人民共和国外交部网站. Last modified November 5, 2019. www.fmprc.gov.cn/zflt/eng/zyzl/hywj/t280369.htm.
9   Author, No. "East China Sea Gas Field in Full Output: CNOOC." *The Japan Times*. Last modified August 5, 2006. www.japantimes.co.jp/news/2006/08/05/national/east-china-sea-gas-field-in-full-output-cnooc/#.XcHWiZJKi_s.
10 "Exclusive: China in $5 Billion Drive to Develop Disputed East China Sea Gas." *U.S.* Last modified July 17, 2013. http://reuters.com/article/us-cnooc-eastchinasea-idUSBRE96G0BA20130717.
11 Plafker, Ted. "A Year Later, China's Stimulus Package Bears Fruit." *The New York Times: Breaking News, World News & Multimedia*. Last modified October 22, 2009. www.nytimes.com/2009/10/23/business/global/23iht-rglobalchin.html.
12 Men, J. *Will the Financial Crisis Make China a Superpower?* Last modified November 9, 2018. www.nato.int/docu/review/2009/financialcrisis/Financial-Crisis-China/EN/index.htm.

13 "China Profile." *BBC News*. Last modified July 29, 2019. www.bbc.com/news/world-asia-pacific-13017882.

14 McCurry, Justin. "China Overtakes Japan as World's Second-Largest Economy." *The Guardian*. Last modified November 26, 2017. www.theguardian.com/business/2011/feb/14/china-second-largest-economy.

15 "China Profile." *BBC News*. Last modified July 29, 2019. www.bbc.com/news/world-asia-pacific-13017882.

16 "China Profile." *BBC News*. Last modified July 29, 2019. www.bbc.com/news/world-asia-pacific-13017882.

17 World Economic Forum Report. http://www3.weforum.org/docs/WEF_Future_of_Consumption_in_Fast_Growth_Consumer_Markets_China.pdf.

18 Amadeo, Kimberly. "3 Types of Free Trade Agreements and How They Work." *The Balance*. Last modified March 10, 2011. www.thebalance.com/free-trade-agreement-types-and-examples-3305897.

19 "China FTA Network." Last modified November 5, 2019. http://fta.mofcom.gov.cn/english/index.shtml.

20 World Economic Forum Report. http://www3.weforum.org/docs/GAC/2014/WEF_GAC_TradeFDI_MegaRegionalTradeAgreements_Report_2014.pdf.

21 Pham, Peter. "Why Did Donald Trump Kill This Big Free Trade Deal?" *Forbes*. Last modified December 29, 2017. www.forbes.com/sites/peterpham/2017/12/29/why-did-donald-trump-kill-this-big-free-trade-deal/#565a37344e62.

22 Gearan, Anne, and David Nakamura. "Hillary Clinton Comes Out against Obama's Pacific Trade Deal." *The Washington Post*. Last modified October 7, 2015. www.washingtonpost.com/news/worldviews/wp/2018/04/13/a-timeline-of-trumps-complicated-relationship-with-the-tpp/.

23 Chen, Yawen, and Ryan Woo. "Citing Trade Tensions, IMF Cuts China's 2019 GDP Growth Forecast to 6.2% from 6.3%." *U.S.* Last modified June 5, 2019. www.reuters.com/article/us-china-economy-imf/citing-trade-tensions-imf-cuts-chinas-2019-gdp-growth-forecast-to-6-2-from-6-3-idUSKCN1T60MP.

24 Lee, Yen Nee. "US and China Could Sign 'Phase One' Trade Deal before Christmas, Pimco Predicts." *CNBC*. Last modified November 19, 2019. www.cnbc.com/2019/11/19/us-china-could-sign-phase-one-trade-deal-before-christmas-pimco-says.html.

25 Cronin, Patrick M., opinion contributor. "US-China Trade Deal: What It Is, Is Not, and May Become." *The Hill*. Last modified October 12, 2019. https://thehill.com/opinion/finance/465546-us-china-trade-deal-what-it-is-is-not-and-may-become.

26 Cronin, Patrick M., opinion contributor. "US-China Trade Deal: What It Is, Is Not, and May Become." *The Hill*. Last modified October 12, 2019. https://thehill.com/opinion/finance/465546-us-china-trade-deal-what-it-is-is-not-and-may-become.

27 Swanson, Ana. "Trump Reaches 'Phase 1' Deal with China and Delays Planned Tariffs." *The New York Times: Breaking News, World News & Multimedia*. Last modified October 12, 2019. www.nytimes.com/2019/10/11/business/economy/us-china-trade-deal.html.

28 Brunnstrom, David, and Matt Spetalnick. "Exclusive: U.S.-China Trade Deal Signing Could Be Delayed Until December." *U.S.* Last modified November 6, 2019. www.reuters.com/article/us-usa-trade-china-prospects-exclusive/exclusive-u-s-china-trade-deal-signing-could-be-delayed-until-december-u-s-source-idUSKBN1XG2GG.

Chapter 3

Shipping and China Ocean Shipping Company

Even though European nations consider themselves as the leaders in the international shipping industry, China had its golden age much earlier. During 1300–1400, the Chinese had sailing ships three times larger than those built by the British who would not catch up until the 1800s.[1] Moreover, due to the seasonal monsoons and years of studying the climate and ocean events, Chinese mariners were able to travel further with little or no additional effort.

During the 1400s, China owned what is known as China's "Treasure Fleet," which consisted of approximately 3,500 ships.[2] By 1525, all of the ships were either burnt or abandoned and eventually rotted. There are various explanations about why this happened but one of the most probable ones was that the land war against the Mongols destroyed the Chinese empire. During the following centuries, the country's shipping would never go back to what it had been. In 1886, the biggest part of China's merchant fleet was sold to Russell & Co.[3] The sale of the fleet marked the end of one of China's steps toward industrial progress.[4] From then and until China's modern Chinese shipping era (1949–to date), China almost completely retreated from a maritime role[5] and focused on land matters. Modern Chinese shipping is divided into two key periods: 1949–1978 and 1978–to date.

All political and economic events discussed in the previous chapter have impacted the formation of China's shipping industry. Today, China is one of the leading ship-owning countries in the world. When the People's Republic of China was founded, however, this was not the case. Prior to 1949, the shipping industry was privately owned and operated. Since its foundation, the People's Republic was economically isolated and had very few diplomatic relations with noncommunist countries. China was influenced by the former USSR model, and all private shipowners were forced to forfeit control of their companies to the state. Moreover, the government set mandatory production goals and companies were subject to government controls. In addition to following their model, China received extensive economic and technical support by various communist states, primarily the former USSR. Few matters were treated and perceived as important as the shipping industry. The Chinese government expected that the industry would be able to satisfy its own foreign trade and that dependence on foreign flag vessels would significantly drop. Moreover, shipping due to its international nature was perceived as a way to develop diplomatic relations with other countries. Finally, by developing its maritime industry, China aimed to build up and establish a strong international position.

Due to policies adopted by the regime, however, diplomatic and commercial relations were primarily with communist countries. Western countries, on the other hand, imposed an embargo on products coming from or going to China, which lasted until the end of the 1950s. Meanwhile, the Chinese government established various shipping services during the early part of the decade. In addition to the newly established companies, the Chinese government aimed to further develop the industry. To do so, any Chinese national living abroad involved in shipping could act as private agents for seagoing vessels. At the beginning of the decade, the Chinese government formed its first international cooperation with Poland. In 1951, the two countries set up the Chinese–Polish Joint Stock Shipping Co., with presence in both countries. A few years later, in 1954, China signed an agreement with Czechoslovakia granting them full powers to operate and purchase vessels for the Chinese Government.[6] Through these agreements and other measures, the Chinese government saw economic growth in the country's maritime trade. Despite the over fivefold increase in Chinese shipping tonnage, trading still greatly depended on foreign carriers.[7]

The 1957 shipping recession caused both freight costs of leasing vessels and the revenue from liner operations to significantly drop. The Chinese government reacted by protecting its interests and demanding the annulment of tariffs on Chinese cargos. By the end of the decade, tariffs on the Far East/European lines had dropped significantly. Furthermore, the end of the decade also meant the beginning of shipbuilding in the Republic. Even though the industry was constantly developing in favor of the

Chinese, expenses in foreign currency were still high due to the chartering of foreign flag vessels.

To lower said expenses and potentially profit from the industry, it was necessary to build a national fleet. The government's additional desire to make the Chinese flag a powerful one led to the creation of a national shipping company. It was on April 27, 1961, that COSCO was founded in Beijing. Almost immediately after its founding, the company's branch in Guangzhou operated a fleet of 25 vessels. Three years later, the Shanghai branch opened. It was clear from the first years of its operation that COSCO would fundamentally contribute to the country's economic development.

In 1964, the Chinese government decided to purchase second-hand vessels to grow the country's fleet. To further encourage the growth of the fleet, the government designed a new, sympathetic policy. First, vessels would have priority in the allocation of exports and imports as well as in all Chinese ports for loading and unloading. Another benefit was that for the first five years the companies did not have to pay neither the loan principal nor interest. An additional motivation was tax exemption until the loan taken to buy or build a vessel was fully repaid. In addition to the government's policy, COSCO established a supplementary policy. Succinctly stated, the company's policy was to obtain loans to purchase vessels and then repay those loans using profits. The first COSCO-owned vessel to sail was MV DUN HUANG in May 1967.

The next decade was of great significance for the company because it opened two new branches and attracted the world's attention by surpassing a 5 million deadweight tonnage (DWT) fleet capacity.[8] Moreover, the first Chinese container liner started operating from Shanghai to Sydney. At the end of the 1970s, a COSCO vessel was scheduled to arrive in Seattle, marking the first Chinese commercial vessel to call at a US port since the establishment of the People's Republic of China. By the end of 1978, the country was no longer relying on leasing foreign vessels and was almost completely independent on its own resources.

The Chinese shipping industry grew significantly within the first 20 years of the country's establishment, and so did COSCO. The company made it clear from the beginning that it aimed to become a superpower within the industry and on January 1, 1980, COSCO established its first joint venture with Holland Parker Boat Group in Rotterdam.[9] Toward the end of the 1980s, COSCO UK was established marking transnational operations which led to the founding of COSCO Europe in 1989. For all this to be possible, as well as for what was coming, the company underwent significant reforming and restructuring.

In 1961, COSCO was established as a *state-owned enterprise* (SOE) and was under the control of the Ocean Shipping Bureau of the *Ministry of Communication* (MOC). This defined the company's identity. COSCO was the government department in matters of developing and implementing maritime policies. Moreover, this role made the company responsible to not only manage the existing shipping industry but also assist in developing it. COSCO had become the country's ambassador in the signing of various international shipping agreements as well as in negotiations with foreign governments and coordinating ship acquisitions.[10]

COSCO simultaneously was the only shipping company upon which all of China depended for the transportation of products. Once the company's first foreign branched opened, its dual identity became an inconvenience. Because the company was part of the government, it had very little power over its policies on prices and investments, and it had limited commercial freedom.

As the Chinese maritime industry grew, it became clear to all parties that certain reforms were necessary. The MOC took the first step in 1982, when it closed the Ocean Shipping Bureau, one of the first departments established since the country's foundation. In a process that lasted two years, COSCO took control of its commercial activities, internal structure, and strategies. The MOC no longer retained control over COSCO operations and was transformed into an administrative and regulatory department. The new, allegedly independent company's first goal was, naturally, to minimize unnecessary expenses. To do so, each of its branches was assigned management of specific fleet types and routes.

For example, COSCO Shanghai was responsible for the container and general cargo ships sailing to the Americas and Oceania as well as specific regions of Asia. Through this seemingly simple restructure, the company's efficiency increased significantly affecting both the company and the country as a whole.

By 1990, the Chinese maritime business had expanded in oceangoing shipping as well as coastal and inland transport companies. During the 1990s, COSCO established various branches worldwide and for the first time funded the construction of Chinese-flag vessels using funds generated overseas. To facilitate further growth, the government increased the number of domestic ports as well as those on foreign soil. Moreover, up until the end of the 1980s, the Chinese government would only permit the transportation of national products in national vessels. It abandoned this policy in 1988 in order to cooperate with international policies. The Chinese and international shipping industry marked a significant milestone in 1992 when China allowed foreign companies to establish sister companies through bilateral agreement for activities in the business of shipping.[11] Furthermore, during the same year, the Chinese government allowed foreigners to establish independent companies within Chinese territory as long as they complied with requirements established by the Chinese government. In addition to this, in July of the same year, China allowed foreigners to operate in Chinese ports. Clearly, China was creating a framework to allow for more open and friendly trade conditions with not only its allies but also the Western world. Furthermore, China enacted policies regarding the development of existing or new ports.

The decade was also significant for COSCO's internal affairs. As the industry evolved, it was clear that the once functional management and operational system needed to be changed. The first modification, to unify the management of the various branches, happened in 1992, and by 1993, the company had enhanced its competitiveness. In 1994, COSCO Industry Corporation was established. The branch's main focus included but was not limited to ship repairs and container manufacture. While the Group was constantly growing, in 1997 various branches were merged. Moreover, COSCO International Freight Forwarding expanded to 303 locations throughout China. During this period of reforming, the group's revenues increased by more than 35%.[12]

In January 2000, during the 30th World Economic Forum (WEF), COSCO was officially enrolled as a member. This was a milestone for both the group and the country since it became the first Chinese company to ever be a member of the WEF. COSCO continued expanding and becoming increasingly more important, evidenced by the fact that the Executive Vice President of the group was voted deputy of the National People's Congress (NPC).

During 2000–2019, the company experienced several milestones, including being listed for the first time in the Fortune Global 500. In 2005, COSCO entered into a historic agreement for the shipping industry with Hyundai Heavy Industries Co., Ltd, to build four 10,000 TEU class super post-panamax containerships, the first of which was delivered only two years later.[13] On May 24, 2006, Jia Qinglin, the Chairman of the Standing Committee of China's NPC, was on an official visit to Greece to examine one of COSCO's vessels at the Port of Piraeus. On August 6, 2014, COSCO

International bought 51% equity interest of Yuan Hua in the United States. By doing so they established a global service network in spare parts supply.[14] On November 4, 2019, COSCO and Jotun A/S, the Norwegian chemicals company, renewed the shareholder agreement for Jotun COSCO Marine Coatings and currently hold 50% of the equity.[15]

Currently, COSCO has established itself in 79 countries and has built a network of 154 worldwide branch offices. Of them, 69 are located out of China and nine within. COSCO's somewhat aggressive expansion abroad represents China's strategy to expand its influence around the world. Moreover, the company operates 332 international and domestic routes, covering a total of 254 ports.[16] COSCO is a constantly growing company, which currently owns 1,307 vessels having an aggregate capacity of 105.44 million DWT.[17] COSCO, including its container fleet, is ranked third after APM-MAERSK and MSC. Other fleets, such as dry bulk and tanker fleets, are all ranked at the top of the global list.

To further establish itself within the international maritime trade, COSCO is a member in the Ocean Alliance, launched in April 2017, which consists of four members, CMA CGM, COSCO Shipping, Evergreen, and OOCL.[18] The aim of the alliance is to bring the *"largest service on the Transpacific trade"*[19] as well as improve services between Asia and Europe, the United States, Gulf of Mexico, and the Red Sea area. Earlier this year, the member companies of the Ocean Alliance signed an extension until 2027, making this ten-year partnership official.[20]

The importance of the alliance is indisputable as it will significantly cut down shipping time. *Maritime Gateway*, south Asia's premier maritime business magazine, estimates that a trip between Busan and New York will only take 22 days and that new, direct services will link Southeast Asia and the United States.[21] Moreover, the alliance will offer the costumers of its members land solutions, such as rail and trucks, within all countries they are present in.

This rather modern trajectory of COSCO's journey is deep-rooted in the historical trade routes of the region, which shaped the world for COSCO to thrive and exist as it does. A look into the historical journey of trade is critical to understanding the seemingly natural success of the development of China's shipping infrastructure and industry, including its poster child for that success, COSCO. After all, the journey to sea inevitably starts at land.

NOTES

1 Vineyard, Jared. "Freight History: China and International Shipping." *Universal Cargo.* Last modified February 9, 2018. www.universalcargo.com/freight-history-china-and-international-shipping/.

2 Edwards, Jim. "500 Years Ago, China Destroyed Its World-Dominating Navy Because Its Political Elite Was Afraid of Free Trade." *Business Insider.* Last modified February 26, 2017. www.businessinsider.com/china-zhenge-he-treasure-fleet-elite-free-trade-2017-2.

3 Russell & Co: The American trading house was the largest in China in the mid-19th century and founded in 1824 by Samuel Russell and primarily traded opium, silk and tea. In 1891, due to financial difficulties the company devolved into Shewan & Company.

4 "China and Maritime Nations, Sea Captains, Merchants, Merchandise, Passengers: 1800–1899." *The Maritime Heritage Projects: Ships, Captains, Merchants, Passengers to 1800s San Francisco.* n.d. Last modified November 6, 2019. https://maritimeheritage.org/ports/china.html.

5 Schottenhammer, Angela. "The 'China Seas' in World History: A General Outline of the Role of Chinese and East Asian Maritime Space from Its Origins to C. 1800." *ScienceDirect.com | Science, Health and Medical Journals, Full Text Articles and Books.* Last modified November 6, 2019. www.sciencedirect.com/science/article/pii/S2212682112000261.

6 Lee, Tae Woo [and others]. *Shipping in China.* Burlington: Ashgate, 2002.

7 Lee, Tae Woo [and others]. *Shipping in China.* Burlington: Ashgate, 2002.

8 Ramburuth, Prem, Christina Stringer, and Manuel Serapio. *Dynamics of International Business: Asia-Pacific Business Cases.* Cambridge: Cambridge University Press, 2013.

9 Xiwen, Xu, and Michael W. Hansen. "The Arrival of Chinese Investors in Denmark: A Survey of Recent Trends in Chinese FDI in Denmark." *Centre for Business and Development Studies.* Last modified August 7, 2017. https://pdfs.semanticscholar.org/9341/a00906192ab5d7e815512b4d98b9d7a4b25a.pdf.

10 Lee, Tae Woo [and others]. *Shipping in China.* Burlington: Ashgate, 2002.

11 Lee, Tae Woo [and others]. *Shipping in China.* Burlington: Ashgate, 2002.

12 Lee, Tae Woo [and others]. *Shipping in China.* Burlington: Ashgate, 2002.

13 "HHI Builds Korea's First 10,000teu Containership." *Seatrade Maritime.* Last modified July 27, 2007. www.seatrade-maritime.com/asia/hhi-builds-koreas-first-10000teu-containership.

14 "Milestones." *COSCO SHIPPING.* Last modified November 25, 2019. www.coscointl.com/en/about-us/cosco-shipping-international/about-milestones/.

15 "Shareholder Agreement Renewed between COSCO SHIPPING International Hong Kong and Jotun A/S." *COSCO SHIPPING.* Last modified November 25, 2019. www.coscointl.com/en/media-centre/news-release/shareholder-agreement-renewed-between-cosco-shipping-international-hong-kong-and-jotun-as/.

16 "COSCO Global." *COSCO.* Last modified November 6, 2019. www.coscoshipping.gr/cosco-global/.

17 "China COSCO Shipping Group Profile." *China COSCO Shipping.* Last modified November 6, 2019. http://en.coscocs.com/col/col6918/index.html.

18 "Ocean Alliance Gets Extended Until 2027." *World Maritime News.* Last modified November 6, 2019. https://worldmaritimenews.com/archives/268878/ocean-alliance-gets-extended-until-2027/.

19 "Ocean Alliance Unveils Day 3 Product." *The Maritime Executive.* Last modified November 6, 2019. www.maritime-executive.com/article/ocean-alliance-unveils-day-3-product.

20 "Ocean Alliance: The World's Largest Operational Agreement between Shipping Companies Is Extended Until 2027." *SHIPFIN Trade Finance.* Last modified November 6, 2019. www.cma-cgm.com/news/2379/ocean-alliance-the-world-s-largest-operational-agreement-between-shipping-companies-is-extended-until-2027.

21 "OCEAN Alliance the Most Important Operational Alliance." *Maritime Gateway.* Last modified April 3, 2017. www.maritimegateway.com/ocean-alliance-important-operational-alliance/.

Chapter 4

Silk Road

The need as well as the desire to exchange goods within and amongst societies is evident throughout human history. To facilitate this need to trade, civilizations have explored different routes by land, by sea and, much later, by air. One of the main goals has always been to maximize the efficiency of these routes in order to maximize profit or, in previous years, return with the most useful or profitable goods. In early human history, some of the most common goods traded from West to East were gold and silver as well as animals and slaves, whereas from East to West, goods such as silk, spices, medicine, and rice as well as paper and gunpowder were amongst the most popular items.[1] As trade between Eastern and Western nations was of great importance and interest to all involved, it is of no surprise that specific routes were developed, the most well-known being the Silk Road.

The establishment of the Silk Road happened gradually over two millenniums ago. Many believe that the Silk Road was established as a trade route during the Han Dynasty. Its major routes, however, were there many years prior and known as the Persian Royal Road. When Alexander the Great came to power in 336 BC, he was familiar with and admired the Persians' strategy in battle. Moreover, they were known to him for their love of wellbeing and their indulgence of luxury. It was no surprise, therefore, when he decided to lead the Macedonian army east. After conquering Asia Minor, Syria, and Egypt, he moved further east and continued as far as the Indian Punjab.

One of Alexander's main policies and ideologies was that there was no point in further expanding if you could not defend what is already yours. This view also adopted by the Chinese, whose expansion policies had them facing the people of the steppes. Once settled in, the Macedonians were introduced to the ancient trade routes used by the locals. It was through them that the Persians were provided with the luxurious (exotic to the Macedonians) products such as silk and spices. The routes, however, facilitated not only the trade of goods but also the interaction of cultures. The Persian and central Asian influence is evident throughout Macedonian and Greek history. Similarly, the Greek presence and influence are evident throughout the area, even after Alexander's death. Even in the Eurasian steppes, miles away from Alexander's empire, funerary objects were found artistically influenced and inspired from Greece.[2]

The steppes played a crucial part in the establishment and expansion of the Silk Road. During the Han Dynasty, the Chinese borders expanded significantly and connected Asia. Networks and routes that were previously almost impregnable were now part of the Silk Road. One of the most representative examples was the route controlled by the Yuezhi and the Xiongnu.

These two nomadic tribes were believed to be blocking the passages connecting China to India and therefore the Western world. During the Han Dynasty trade with both tribes, especially the Xiongnu, was vital to the Chinese empire. According to Han authors,[3] numerous cattle were bought from the people in the steppes. The tribes were providing the empire with horses needed to maintain stability both internally and against foreign threats. Ironically, what they considered the biggest foreign threat were those providing them with a crucial part of their defense mechanism. The Chinese would exchange their most valuable goods for the horses.

To have a stable and reliable trading route, peace must be ensured. Peaceful relations between the empire and the nomads were not always easy. According to some historians, the Xiongnu tribe was unpredictable and ferocious. On the other hand, the Chinese believed in their superiority and had already developed the concept of Huaxia.[4] During the first years, the intentions of the Han Dynasty were clear, they had chosen peace over war. To do so, they established a formal system of tribute, by some also considered to be bribery. The most common goods that the Han offered in return for peace were rice and wine. However, the most valuable item was silk, considered a symbol of political and social power by the nomads. They used it as both bedding and clothing due to its lightness and texture.

It was not long before some viewed this relationship as China's political weakness. The empire allowed other neighboring tribes to believe that by the threat of instability they would gain the same privileges as the Xiongnu. The first thing the Han emperors had to establish was control over the fertile grounds of the tribe. It took the Chinese a decade to take control over the Gansu corridor, a strategic location within the empire. Moreover, during these years they also expanded to the Pamir Mountains, which were then the passage to the Western world. The empire's success in conquering this new territory and opening new routes is considered the birth of the Silk Road.

The routes, however, were neither readily accessible nor always safe. The available passages at the time were through the Taklamakan Desert, through the Tian Shan Mountains, or through the Pamirs, all character- ized by extreme weather conditions. Inaccessibility and treacherous con- ditions were some of the main reasons trade between China and the rest of the world did not start overnight. Evaluating the risks associated with the journey, merchants would make sure that the rewards were worthy. Although items of low value, such as bamboo and Sichuan cloth, were documented to have been transported via those routes, merchants mostly transported goods of high value.

One of the most valuable goods at the time was silk. During the Han Dynasty, silk was not only an international luxury item but also used as a form of currency to pay the soldiers in remote areas. Another unexpected use of silk has been documented in Central Asia in a Buddhist monastery where monks who had broken any foundational rules would pay their fine in silk.[5]

Irrespective of the route the merchants picked in order to reach the empire, once they started the journey they had to stick to the designated routes. Moreover, Chinese officials would document all visitors entering or leaving the country. This was a way to ensure that all visitors had left the country. Another benefit the Chinese saw in this restrictive policy was that they were able to better document the value of goods that were traded in the country.

Another empire that had a fundamental role in the establishment of, and which greatly used the Silk Road, was the Roman empire. The Roman emperors were aware of the immense possibilities of conquering the east meant, as they also knew the limitations of Europe. After the empire's establishment in Egypt, expeditions were begun to further discover and understand the eastern world. It was under Augustus that Roman soldiers reached today's Ethiopia and Yemen.

Around that time, Isidorus of Charax, put together a transcript known as Σταθμοί Παρθικοί (Stathmoi Parthikoi), a transcript documenting distances and important commercial locations to the East, reaching to Afghanistan.[6] The document also recorded goods exchanged via these paths. Trade between the Roman Empire and further east was one of the primary activities. According to the historian, philosopher, and geographer Strabo, 120 ships were sailing yearly from the empire's ports in the Red Sea to India.[7]

We know that Romans traded local products in western India, including but not limited to spices and precious gems; however, India served another purpose for the Romans, too. It was the maritime gate to and from central and Southeast Asia. Archeological excavations have shown that various items originating from the area made their way to Egypt. Similarly, products exclusively produced in the Red Sea area have been discovered in both central and southeastern regions.

One of the most controversial goods to arrive in Rome was Chinese silk. On the one hand, due to its origin and luxurious feel, it was used as a sign of wealth. On the other hand, for many old-fashioned Romans, silk was provocative and a representation of a newly rising social class.[8] Due to the new trading routes, many merchants were able to accumulate wealth and be part of the high class.

As networks expanded and trade thrived, villages got bigger and towns were transformed into cities. The influence of the Roman Empire was so profound that even local coins were shaped and inspired by those used in the empire. Ports in the Kushan Territory are clear examples of this, especially Barygaza, located in northwestern India. Even though the port was in one of the most dangerous locations, it was a well-established trading point. Due to the strong currents, both approaching and calling the port was challenging for the experienced mariners and almost impossible for the inexperienced. The locals, however, not wanting to lose the benefits of trade would send out pilots to assist and guide the ships to berth. Westerners saw the importance of the port in that goods gathered there from all over central Asia and China.

Although goods were constantly imported and exported to China from the west, there was no direct contact between Chinese and western merchants. Moving from one city to another took much longer than it does today, and the physical impact on individuals was much greater. Most merchants had to walk from one location to another under all weather conditions. Because of such conditions as well as the nature of the paths they had to cross and assuming that an individual walks 5 km/hour, it is likely that they did not walk for much more than 1–2 hours at this speed.[9] Therefore, especially when talking about perishable goods, merchants would trade within a radius of 50 km.[10]

This, however, changed under the Qin Dynasty, during the first century AD. General Ban Chao led expeditions to the west arriving all the way at the Caspian Sea and gathering information. Since the Chinese Empire was known to have precious gems, gold, and silver, Persian traders were eager to establish relations. It was through them that Romans started interacting with the Chinese. As the world was evolving so did trade. Moving the Roman capital from Rome to somewhere more to the east had been discussed under various emperors. It was Emperor Constantine in AD 324, who made this happen.

The new capital, Constantinople, was located in the merging point of Europe and Asia, on the bunks of the Bosporus. By creating the eastern capital, Constantine had created a stronger empire that eventually survived Rome by several centuries, the Byzantine Empire. Due to its location, the empire's capital controlled both sea and land routes to the West. Moreover, it was significantly closer to the Caspian Sea and to other established routes connecting to the East and especially China. It is of no surprise, therefore, that merchants from all over Europe were setting up trading posts at Constantinople. Various European traders and explorers departed from Constantinople hoping that their cherished products would reach China. The most well-known, and probably one of the very few, was Marco Polo and his family. A detailed analysis of their journey stops proves that the routes used then are very similar to the ones that will probably be used in the OBOR initiative. Moreover, the important contrast of the time consumed then and now can be drawn.

Originally from the Republic of Venice, Marco was born into a family of traders. Both his father and his uncle had traveled and visited many of the Eastern countries, including China. But the longest trip they took was with Marco, who then published a book about it. The Polo family accompanied by two friars, who abandoned them soon, started making their way to the East in 1271. The two men had traveled in the past, they followed a different path. Their trip can be divided into parts. The first one was crossing Eurasian territory. Going North into Caucasus, Georgia, and Armenia, they arrived at Tabriz. The city attracted merchants from many regions due to the versatility of the available goods. Marco Polo described the city as a cultural and commercial center, attributing its characteristics to its geographical location. In addition to their location, it is believed that trade was flourishing in these areas due to the minorities living there. It was because of their family ties and common customs that a network of credit was created and successful even over long distances.

The second part of the Polos' journey was from Tabriz to Badakhshan. Instead of going directly to Badakhshan, they headed south to Hormuz, a port in south Iran. Their initial plan was to travel by sea to the Chinese coast. This however did not happen so they headed back north. During this part of the journey, they passed by various places in Iran until reaching their destination. Located in the heart of the Silk Road, trade of silk and precious gems was flourishing. After a year there, the Polo family was ready to continue further north past the Pamir Mountains and Taklamakan desert. Upon their arrival, the Polos were traversing important trading locations and approaching China.

After facing the extreme mountain and desert weather conditions, the Polos, just like the many other merchants, had to face the Gobi Desert. Along this path, they stopped in various cities, all equally important in the Silk Road and the trading network. The importance of this route is suggested through Marco Polo's writing, as he describes it as one commonly used despite the absence of food. Following the rough journey through the desert, the Polos arrived to Suchow.

The city was one of the major cities in the area and of great importance to the southern Silk Road Network. The city's importance was not only due to the Silk Road. Located in today's Gansu Province, the road connecting India, Mongolia, and southern Siberia passed through it. Moreover, the city was at the entrance to the Hexi Corridor, the most important route connecting North and Central China.

The family's final destination, however, was not yet reached. After spending a year in Suchow and four years since the commencement of their journey, the Polos finally arrived at Kublai Khan's summer residence. The first meeting with the Khan as well as the years Marco Polo spent with him forms a significant and detailed part of Polo's book. Marco Polo continued traveling in various cities of the Silk Road network as a representative of the Khan.

After 17 years of services, the Polos had one last task and then they would finally head back to Venice. They had to escort a princess to Persia, a trip that would last two years. Marco Polo wrote very little on the sailing experience to Hormuz. The ship sailed from South China to Sumatra, continuing through the Indian Ocean to finally arrive in the Persian Gulf. During the two years onboard, conditions were rough and many of the passengers and crew died.

Upon the completion of their last task, the Polos headed, by land, northwest. Once they reached the Black Sea, they boarded a ship at Trebizond.

They sailed through Constantinople and then continued to Venice, where they finally arrived in 1295. Their total trip lasted 24 years, during which they traveled through all the major points of the Silk Road by both land and sea. Moreover, they gathered goods and experiences from various major trading points. However, the most important accomplishment was Marco Polo's book "Livres des Merveilles du Monde."[11] It is because of his work that information about traveling the Silk Road and the trading network has not been lost and can be applied today as historical context to the development of OBOR.

Marco Polo and his family were probably amongst some of the last travelers to use the Silk Road networks to such an extent. Even before commencing their trip the network was already in decay. As the Roman Empire started losing power many nomadic tribes started gaining power. The time of transition made the areas increasingly unstable and unsafe. Therefore, routes that were once popular and cities that were hubs became less appealing to merchants. This was the first sign of the decline of the network. A few decades later, the fall of the Tang Dynasty triggered the rapid decline of the land network. As land transport became increasingly unsafe and unreliable, sea transportation rose. Moreover, most of the Silk Road network was based on the need of intermediaries to transport the goods. Due to the rise of sea transport, most middlemen were eliminated, because sea transport is, by nature, more direct.

When the Silk Road network collapsed, trading certainly did not follow. Merchants from all ends of the world would meet and trade in various locations. Such activities are, of course, present until today, where the exports and imports do not only define companies but countries as a whole. Moreover, as the main goal, in businesses of all sizes and specializations, is to eliminate the need for middlemen, new networks are being created. One of those networks is the OBOR initiative.

NOTES

1 Frankopan, Peter. "The Creation of the Silk Road." In *The Silk Roads: A New History of the World*, 1–26. New York: Vintage, 2016.

2 Frankopan, Peter. "The Creation of the Silk Road." In *The Silk Roads: A New History of the World*, 1–26. New York: Vintage, 2016.

3 Frankopan, Peter. "The Creation of the Silk Road." In *The Silk Roads: A New History of the World*, 1–26. New York: Vintage, 2016.

4   The concept of huaxia represented the Han Chinese nation and civilization.
5   Lagerwey, John. "Religious Life in a Silk Road Community: Niya During the Third and Fourth Centuries." In *Religion and Chinese Society: Ancient and Medieval China Volume 1*, 279–316. Hong Kong: Chinese University Press, 2004.
6   Electricpulp.com. "Isidorus of Charax: Encyclopaedia Iranica." In *Encyclopædia Iranica | Pages*. n.d. Last modified November 6, 2019. www.iranicaonline.org/articles/isidorus-of-charax.
7   Frankopan, Peter. "The Creation of the Silk Road." In *The Silk Roads: A New History of the World*, 1–26. New York: Vintage, 2016.
8   Frankopan, Peter. "The Creation of the Silk Road." In *The Silk Roads: A New History of the World*. New York: Vintage, 2016.
9   Howard, Lawrence A. "Geographic, Economic, Cultural, and Historical Contexts of Transportation Development." *Lecture, Transportation Management: TMGT 73001*, SUNY Maritime, New York, September 20, 2019.
10 Howard, Lawrence A. "Geographic, Economic, Cultural, and Historical Contexts of Transportation Development." *Lecture, Transportation Management: TMGT 73001*, SUNY Maritime, New York, September 20, 2019.
11 Polo, Marco. *Le livre des merveilles du monde*. Paris: J'ai Lu, 2005.

Chapter 5

One Belt One Road Initiative

Today, many years after Marco Polo's journey and the disappearance of the ancient Silk Road network, the concept of the trade route between east and west appears more present than ever. The *New Silk Roads*, known as the OBOR initiative is, as President Xi stated in May 2017, the project of the century incorporating over 80 countries. The nations included in the OBOR initiative account for over 63% of the world's population, with a collective 29% of total global output.[1]

Of course, such a project cannot be planned overnight and requires significant investment. Moreover, due to the many countries involved and their geopolitical situations, politics and political stability are fundamental. For the past couple of years, however, politics in the Western world have been characterized by anything but stability. Changes in the US political scene as well as in many European countries show a trend of rising nationalism and potentially, though unlikely, deglobalization.

Protection of a nation's sovereignty as well as its borders should, without a doubt, be a priority. However, extreme measures go against some of today's world's basic advantages, according to which goods, money, and people move and cooperate somewhat freely benefiting millions of people around the world.[2] During the past years, conservative leaders and certain populations of voters have been inclined to such measures. President Trump greatly focused his electoral campaign on maligning open immigration as well as the inability of the United States to economically compete with others, like Japan.

Nationalistic views are increasingly shared by parties and political groups in major European countries. In France, for example, Marine Le Pen, daughter of the co-founder of the National Front far-right party who describes the Nazi gas chambers as a mere "detail" in the history of World War II, has gained some popularity. Le Pen's views on not only

35

immigration but also her criticism of the *European Union* (EU) and the Eurozone made her party, National Front, the runner-up in the preliminary round of the 2017 elections. Similarly, in both Germany and Greece, the extreme right parties, Alternative für Deutschland and Χρυσή Αυγή (Golden Dawn), respectively, have gained approval. In the Greek 2015 elections and the German 2017 elections, the aforementioned parties gained seats in the two parliaments for the first time.

Many other member countries have been criticizing the EU under the auspices of an inability to benefit member nations. One of the issues triggering this discontent has been the arrival of refugees and economic migrants. The inability of the EU to assist as well as the constant disagreements between its members have raised questions about its future. The most characteristic example of this new wave was the vote in the United Kingdom in favor of exiting the EU. Boris Johnson, a key supporter of Brexit, alleged that the UK's membership in the EU had severely damaged the nation's economy; thereby highlighting that the EU should not simply be concerned with the Brexit proposition but also the significance. At the minimum, the Brexit alarm, as it is unclear whether the United Kingdom will actually heed its unexpected referendum results, raises criticisms on taken-for-granted agreements and trends that were once perceived by the majority to be beneficial. The Western world, once deemed the center of globalization, is currently not moving as fast as it once was.[3]

On the other hand, the Eastern world is experiencing political and economic collaboration. In sort of a revival of the European dark ages, when the East thrived and the West was breaking down. Since the early 2010s, there are multiple examples of diplomatic advances and partnerships between Asian nations, for example, Turkmenistan and Uzbekistan. In early 2017, the presidents of the two countries inaugurated a new railway bridge across the Amu Darya River, their shared natural border.[4] The project is significant not only for trading between the two nations but also for the region. Turkmenistan and Uzbekistan are only an example of the many projects on which Central Asian countries are working together. Many others are doing the same and governments are investing in common projects.

In fact, ties between seemingly unconnected nations have been forming. Afghanistan and Tajikistan have signed agreements to construct a pipeline benefiting both countries. Similarly, Iran and Azerbaijan seek to engage in a common development in the energy sector. Afghanistan and Tajikistan, however, are in the center of such projects. On the one hand, Afghanistan's Shah Deniz II gas field is now linked to southeastern

Europe through the *Trans-Anatolian Pipeline* (TANAP). Another example of cooperative economic development is that hydroelectric power plants are planned to operate in Tajikistan and Kyrgyzstan and provide power to both Pakistan and Afghanistan by 2020.[5] The aforementioned projects are only a couple of examples of the cooperative trend in the region. In addition to the financial benefits these projects provide, they also foster diplomatic relationships between governments.

Another important partnership currently discussed is that between Iran and the members of the *Eurasian Economic Union* (EAEU). Another project, materializing in recent months, is the *Greater Eurasian Partnership* according to Deputy Director of the Industrial Policy Department of the EAEU, Tigran Harutunyan. During his interview, Mr. Harutunyan said that a number of projects in various locations are now being implemented.[6]

In Belarus, for example, a high-tech zone called the Great Stone Industrial Park is fully operational. The park is located in a strategic location, 25 km from the country's capital, close to both the international airport and railway, and also the transnational highway connecting Berlin to Moscow.

A second example Mr. Harutunyan gave is the Krasnoyarsk Technological Valley in Russia, which some observers see as the Silicon Valley of the East.

Finally, in Kazakhstan, initiatives for some of the largest industrial projects in electronics, light industry, and other industries are being implemented. Whether those projects amongst others are used merely for Russia's and the EAEU's benefit or for the benefit of the OBOR network depends upon China's future actions.

In September 2013, President Xi traveled to Kazakhstan to give a speech at a local university. During his speech, titled "Promote People-to-People Friendship and Create a Better Future," President Xi analyzed the importance and significance of the New Silk Road initiative. Moreover, he said that same would "forge closer economic ties, deepen cooperation and expand development space in the Eurasian region."[7] Such statements were not made for the first time and people from around the world were hesitant to believe in a project of such magnitude. The major difference and what made President Xi's statement believable were that he had readily available cash as well as concrete proposals. By then, it was obvious that a lot of thinking and planning had gone into the matter prior to Xi's speech.

As mentioned in Chapter 2, in the early 2000s, the Chinese government adopted open policies. Moreover, local businesses have been encouraged to find opportunities within and outside Chinese soil. President Xi took advantage of existing policies, created new initiatives, and altered the government's priorities to facilitate his objectives. By early 2016, the *Export–Import Bank of China* was funding more than 1,000 projects across almost 50 countries. These projects as well as the ones to follow were inspired by President Xi's vision for a "new era of harmony and trade."[8] Most importantly, the OBOR initiative provides much-needed hope for new alliances and international cooperation, providing China with a great opportunity to become an even stronger player in the global economy.

China has without a doubt evolved, developed, and become a leading member of the Eastern economic world. Knowing how to emerge from poverty and how to transform cities into major hubs, the Chinese government is investing in highways, railways, and ports among other transportation projects. The *China–Pakistan Economic Corridor* (CPEC) is a great example of both positive and negative outcomes of the initiative. The project involves investments in roads, energy plants as well as a deep-water port at Gwadar. Even though the benefits might appear obvious to many observers, local Pakistani political groups have raised questions about the actual benefits for Pakistanis versus Chinese interests.

One of the major issues, according to Nadeem Akhter's[9] interview with Shamil Shams,[10] is the country's national security. Pakistani military generals are prioritizing defense ties with Beijing. Moreover, another concern is the relationship with neighboring, historical rival India. Chinese and Indian bilateral trade has improved significantly during the past years.[11] Despite this increase, the Indian government chose not to attend the May 2017 Beijing Forum. The reason not to attend was the fact that CPEC passes through Kashmir, which Indian officials assert "violates [India's] territorial integrity."[12]

Azad Jammu and Kashmir, commonly known as Kashmir, is located in the borders of Pakistan, China, and India (see Figure 5.1). It is known for its environmental beauty, including its glaciers. Kashmir provides the area with fresh water, including part of India. Additionally, it serves as a source of power generation for both Pakistan and India. The area is unquestionably of great interest and significance for the OBOR initiative because of its geographical location as a crucial water gateway for China. Additionally, for OBOR, China has strategically chosen and invested into places rich in natural resources; Kashmir falls into this category.[13]

Currently, and in addition to the country's political and military instability, Pakistan is going through a severe economic crisis. It is estimated

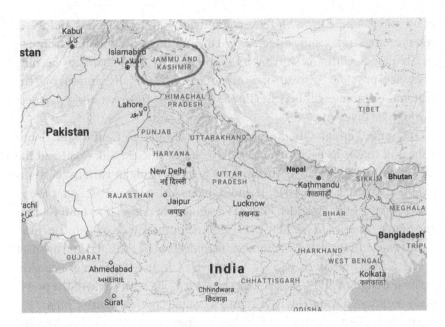

FIGURE 5.1
Map of Jammu and Kashmir.

that through the CPEC Project, China has invested around $60 billion.[14] According to Akhtar's same interview,[15] the investment was welcomed by the previous government and considered as a much-needed one. However, since the newly elected Prime Minister Imran Khan took over, the project *"should be suspended for at least one year"* as minister of commerce, Razaq Dawood, stated in September 2018.[16]

Although Pakistan is unquestionably an important country for the OBOR initiative, security is an important factor for the Chinese to consider. Since it is impossible to guarantee total security and military stability, the Chinese government is constantly analyzing and investing in other proposals. A major project is that of connecting Malaysia's East and West coasts as well as its major ports. The East Coast Rail Line will be part of a greater high-speed and freight-train railway running across Southeast Asia. Projects for deep-water ports are constantly being discussed and executed. Already approved developments are constructed in Bangladesh, Sri Lanka as well as Vietnam, to name a few.[17]

In summary, there are three key motivating factors for China to successfully complete the OBOR initiative. First and most importantly, to meet and satisfy the nation's internal need for natural resources. It is no coincidence that a big percentage of the projects consist of the construction of oil and gas pipelines. Moreover, countries with fertile lands and water reserves are strategically selected for collaboration. Second, and as noted in Chapter 2, China is shifting its economy. The final goal is to become a service provider instead of a manufacturer.[18] Finally, improving the regional economy will benefit China, which sees future trading partners through its investments.

Of course, China's OBOR initiative is not limited to Central and South Asia, and that is a specific contrast between the ancient Silk Road and the modern Chinese initiative. Investments are also made in various locations in South America, such as Chile and Bolivia. Although not as aggressive as in other parts of the world, China has a significant presence in both Central and South America. As of May 2019,[19] seven South American countries have signed the *OBOR-related memoranda of understanding* (MOU) and are part of the OBOR initiative, namely Venezuela, Guyana, Suriname, Ecuador, Bolivia, Uruguay, and Chile. Brazil and Peru along with some of the previously mentioned countries have signed a double tax treaty with China.

Another investment toward the global initiative is COSCO's involvement in the Chancay terminal in Lima, of which they have acquired 60%[20] for $225 million.[21] Moreover, South America, and especially Argentina, is rich in natural resources. It is of no surprise, therefore, that China is funding the infrastructure of two nuclear plants. Additionally, an Argentina–China cooperation project is underway aiming to upgrade the country's main cargo rail network.[22] However, due to the recent elections (October 2019), it is unclear how many of the projects will continue and in what pace.

The aforementioned projects prove that China's ambitions are not restricted to Europe and Asia. The MOUs are primarily signed by the "less powerful" countries of the area, whereas Argentina, Brazil, Peru, and Mexico have yet to sign. Nonetheless, China is establishing its presence in the area. Moreover, the fact that China desires to take powerful stakes in South American economies proves that the OBOR initiative is much larger and more ambitious than the ancient Silk Road network ever was, even for its time.

Because these OBOR projects are still in primitive stages, South American countries are not being officially included into the variations of the OBOR maps.

Some of the initiative's most significant investments have been or will be made in Africa as well as key locations in Europe. The most important of these investments is the completion of the first fully electrified cross-border railway line in Africa, linking Addis Ababa to Djibouti's port. Additional railway projects as well as road infrastructure projects are being built or completed. It is important to point out, however, that not all projects that had been agreed to are likely to be completed. In Sierra Leone, a $318 million airport project was cancelled. The agreement was signed during the previous government led by President Ernest Bai Koroma. However, the new government, led by Julius Maada Bio, observed that "it is uneconomical to proceed with the construction of the new airport when the existing one is grossly underutilized."[23]

A successful investment that has been completed is the Doraleh multipurpose Port in Djibouti. The port was constructed by *China State Construction Engineering Corp* (CSCEC) and costs over $421 million. The port, which has been operating since May 2017, has a handling capacity of 7.08 million tons a year,[24] with both container and oil terminals connected to the Addis Ababa–Djibouti railway. Another important project in Djibouti is the International *Free Trade Zone* (FTZ) that opened in July 2018. The FTZ, which includes China Merchants Holdings, Dalian Port Corp as well as Djibouti Ports, is considered as one of the major links between countries participating in the OBOR initiative. In Europe, China's presence is also noted through various projects, such as the Zeebrugge terminal in Belgium and the Piraeus Port in Greece.

The Piraeus investment and its consequences can be considered China's most significant commercial beach head in Europe in pursuit of OBOR. Because of Greece's geographic location in the eastern Mediterranean, the country historically has long been considered a gateway to Europe.

On the one hand, being the country's main and largest port Piraeus, its development is of great domestic importance to Greece. It is a well-established and busy port, which directly or indirectly provides jobs to many Greeks. On the other hand, the Chinese cannot fail to recognize that Piraeus is the first European port at which a vessel journeying from the East through the Suez Canal can call.

NOTES

1   "A New Future for the World Economy." *HSBC Commercial Banking | HSBC.* Last modified December 3, 2019. www.business.hsbc.com/belt-and-road/a-new-future-for-the-world-economy.

2   "Opinion | When Borders Close." *The New York Times: Breaking News, World News & Multimedia.* Last modified November 12, 2016. www.nytimes.com/2016/11/13/opinion/sunday/when-borders-close.html.

3 "Global Growth Tracker." *World Economics: The Global Authority on Economic Data*. Last modified November 26, 2019. www.worldeconomics.com/%20papers/ Global%20Growth%20Monitor_7c66ffca-ff86-4e4c-979d-7c5d7a22ef21.paper.

4 "Uzbek, Turkmen Presidents Agree to Cooperation on Energy, Transportation, Security." *RadioFreeEurope/RadioLiberty*. Last modified March 6, 2017. www.rferl.org/a/ uzbekistan-turkmenistan-mirziyaev-berdymukhammedov/28354163.html.

5 Yousafzai, Fawad. "Work on CASA-1000 Power Project in Full Swing: Tajik Diplomat." *The Nation*. Last modified July 19, 2018. https://nation.com.pk/19-Jul-2018/ work-on-casa-1000-power-project-in-full-swing-tajik-diplomat.

6 Full interview of Mr. Harutunyan can be found in the Appendix section.

7 Frankopan, Peter. *The New Silk Roads: The Present and Future of the World*. New York: Knopf, 2019.

8 Bosu, Rabi Sankar. "BRI Will Bring China and ASEAN Closer." *China.org.cn: China News, Business, Travel & Language Courses*. Last modified May 22, 2017. www.china. org.cn/opinion/2017-05/22/content_40865507.htm.

9 Nadeen Akhtar is a Karachi-based political commentator, author and columnist.

10 Shams, Shamil. "Belt and Road Forum: Is the China-Pakistan Economic Corridor Failing?" *DW.COM*. Last modified November 7, 2019. www.dw.com/en/ belt-and-road-forum-is-the-china-pakistan-economic-corridor-failing/a-48473486.

11 Rajagopalan, Rajeswari Pillai. "Are China-India Relations Really Improving?" *The Diplomat: The Diplomat Is a Current-Affairs Magazine for the Asia-Pacific, with News and Analysis on Politics, Security, Business, Technology and Life across the Region*. Last modified March 1, 2018. https://thediplomat.com/2018/03/ are-china-india-relations-really-improving/.

12 Xin, Zhang. "Indian Ambassador to China Optimistic about Future of Bilateral Relations." *Global Times*. Last modified January 25, 2018. www.globaltimes.cn/content/ 1086596.shtml.

13 Illustration from: "Jammu and Kashmir." *Jammu and Kashmir*. Last modified December 8, 2019. www.google.com/maps/place/Jammu+and+Kashmir/@33.0469 992,73.4518625,6.35z/data=!4m5!3m4!1s0x38e1092499ffa89d:0x6567a6d4697e7f1! 8m2!3d33.778175!4d76.5761714.

14 Toppa, Sabrina. "Why Young Pakistanis Are Learning Chinese." *The Atlantic*. Last modified November 14, 2018. www.theatlantic.com/international/archive/2018/11/ pakistan-china-cooperation-cpec/568750/.

15 Shams, Shamil. "Belt and Road Forum: Is the China-Pakistan Economic Corridor Failing?" *DW.COM*. Last modified November 7, 2019. www.dw.com/en/ belt-and-road-forum-is-the-china-pakistan-economic-corridor-failing/a-48473486.

16 Shams, Shamil. "Belt and Road Forum: Is the China-Pakistan Economic Corridor Failing?" *DW.COM*. Last modified November 7, 2019. www.dw.com/en/ belt-and-road-forum-is-the-china-pakistan-economic-corridor-failing/a-48473486.

17 Frankopan, Peter. *The New Silk Roads: The Present and Future of the World*. New York: Knopf, 2019.

18 Frankopan, Peter. *The New Silk Roads: The Present and Future of the World*. New York: Knopf, 2019.

19 Devonshire-Ellis, Chris. "China's Belt & Road Initiative and South America." *Silk Road Briefing*. Last modified June 13, 2019. www.silkroadbriefing.com/news/2019/05/29/ chinas-belt-road-initiative-south-america/.

20 "COSCO Shipping Ports Buys Stake in Peruvian Chancay Terminal." *World Maritime News*. Last modified November 7, 2019. https://worldmaritimenews.com/archives/269604/cosco-shipping-ports-buys-stake-in-peruvian-chancay-terminal/.

21 "China's Belt & Road Initiative and South America." *Silk Road Briefing*. Last modified June 13, 2019. www.silkroadbriefing.com/news/2019/05/29/chinas-belt-road-initiative-south-america/.

22 Gonzalez, Joaquin V. "Argentine Cargo Rail Network Witnesses Great Improvements with China's Help: World: Chinadaily.com.cn." *Global Edition*. Last modified January 18, 2019. www.chinadaily.com.cn/a/201901/18/WS5c419473a3106c65c34e54d7.html.

23 Chaudhury, Dipanjan Roy. "Africa Cancels a Belt and Road Initiative Project for the First Time." *The Economic Times*. Last modified October 25, 2018. https://economictimes.indiatimes.com/news/international/world-news/africa-cancels-a-bri-project-for-the-first-time/articleshow/66363312.cms.

24 *China Daily*. "Belt and Road: Past, Present and Future." *The Telegraph*. Last modified May 2, 2019. www.telegraph.co.uk/china-watch/business/belt-road-projects-list/.

Chapter 6

Possible OBOR Routes and Their Concerns

All of the projects discussed in the previous chapter seem to be scattered around the world and fairly independent of one another. However, this apparent scatter is illusory because the projects are connected; they depend upon each other to reach their maximum utility for China.

When officials talk about the OBOR initiative, they refer to specific routes, with specific stops, risks, and benefits.[1] According to latest estimations, there are over 100 maps[2] traced with suggested routes. Said routes may be divided into three main categories: the maritime route, the northern land route, and the southern land route. Ideally, circumstances will be such to allow all three of the routes to be safely and efficiently used. Although all have their own difficulties, the Northern route is the hardest and most expensive. On the other hand, the maritime route is the cheapest and the most readily accessible, because it needs the least infrastructure investment, so it becomes a critical option and the primary route to consider.

In fact, the maritime route is already in use. To say that there is a clear starting point would be erroneous. Ports around China, such as Hong Kong, Tianjin, Shanghai, Hainan, and so on, are being considered. Each choice entails different compromises. Hong Kong, for example, is the most popular due to its international assets, but it is also the most costly option. Although cutting expenses is a priority in most companies, OBOR is a state initiative, and Hong Kong presents a major geographical advantage. Located on the Southwestern coast of China, it reduces travel time for ships that depart from it. Moreover, Hong Kong is a major city with all of the necessary infrastructure to support the OBOR initiative.

Hong Kong's main competitor is Hainan, located even more to the west. Although currently developing, the city is nowhere near as large nor as organized as Hong Kong. Of course, the risks associated with such a less international city may be compromised by the significant reduction in expenses. If it is not the port of origin, Hainan will be the first stop as it is the last port in Chinese territory at which a vessel heading west to Europe will be able to call.

Another major city which might be considered as the starting port is Shanghai. The city has always been the center of China's finance and maritime industry. Despite its historical importance, however, its geographical location is a major disadvantage for both the maritime and the Southern land route.

Irrespective of the vessel's origin, the next major port will most probably be Singapore. Singapore has long been a hub for both shipping and banking, attracting companies from all over the world. When the country gained its independence in 1965, it was very different from what it is today, having in only a few decades transformed itself into one of Asia's wealthiest nations.[3] Of course, such transformation was not achieved by chance. By focusing on innovative infrastructure projects, such as the Next Generation Port 2030, and encouraging private sector development by creating an investment-friendly environment, Singapore attracted entities from all over the world. Moreover, Singapore is home to the world's largest transshipment container port,[4] thus making it an inevitable stop within the OBOR maritime route.

After Singapore, vessels traveling the OBOR will probably have two options, either a straight sail to Djibouti or through Sri Lanka, Pakistan, and other neighboring countries. Either way, Chinese vessels will eventually be calling Djibouti for, at least, refueling. To ensure its popularity and in an effort to be up-to-date, construction of liquefied natural gas (LNG) started in March 2016 at Damerjog terminal.[5] From there, it is either a straight line to Europe or South to other African ports. Sailing to Europe through the Suez Canal vessels will be arriving in Turkey or Greece or Italy, depending upon the cargo's final destination. The return trip will be determined by the cargo loaded and unloaded along the journey. Because maximizing profit is a key factor in the shipping industry, the return journey will seek to be as profitable as the outbound journey.

Sailing from China to Europe can include numerous ports, cargos, and dangers. One of the most typical issues mariners will certainly face is that of inclement weather. Sailing the third largest ocean in the world takes time and can hold unforeseen weather conditions, during which vessels might suffer a casualty.

Another important issue is that of piracy. Most vessels are expected to call on the Djibouti port and to do so they must sail through the Gulf of Aden. The area is known for the high pirate activity, as also shown in the map provided by the *International Maritime Bureau* (IMB).[6] The IMB is the division of the International Chamber of Commerce focusing on the fight against maritime crimes, including piracy. The IMB provides advice to masters and a 24/7 anti-piracy helpline. Moreover, through their live map and updates, they provide crews and companies with valuable information on current events. The IMB releases reports on actual and attempted attacks including various tables and narrations of actual events. The IMB is without doubt of great significance for the safety of the maritime community.

Moreover, in the past year, there have been incidents of Global Positioning System (GPS) spoofing recorded in the Arabian Sea. By spoofing the vessel's GPS, the receiver will be deceived and inaccurately estimate the vessel's position.[7] The crew will then observe the wrong data and may, due to an overreliance on e-navigation and the false sense of its accuracy, change the course of the vessel. Observing the wrong GPS signals and deviating from the original sailing route might cause other more severe results for the vessel. For example, depending upon the vessel's flag deviating from its original course might lead to a diplomatic incident. Not all vessels may sail to all waters. There are laws and regulations that limit the ability of a vessel to enter and exit certain zones and permission must be obtained in advance, particularly in hostile areas. Moreover, pirates might spoof the GPS system of a vessel leading it to waters which are under their control. This not only will affect the vessel and its cargo, but also jeopardizes the safety of the crewmembers.

Spoofing a vessel's GPS is not the only form of cyberattack unique to the maritime industry. A jamming attack, which serves to completely block a signal rather than alter it, severely affects a vessel. As a result, the navigation system of a vessel suffers and all systems relying upon the navigation system would collapse. This includes the vessel traffic service (VTS), the automatic identification system (AIS), and the communication system, amongst others, that would be compromised. Without a GPS, the crew must rely exclusively upon manual navigation, visual appreciations of their surroundings, for example, other vessels, sea life, or obstacles, to continue its voyage or to successfully perform maneuvers. As a result, both crew and vessel depend entirely upon the experience of the vessel's Master and its Navigation Officer.

Another major concern of maritime cyberterrorism is the hacking of a vessel's particular AIS instead of spoofing or jamming the full GPS system. Most commercial and passenger vessels use the AIS to locate other ships sailing nearby. By manipulating this system, hackers can either create a phantom ship or make an existing one disappear. This might result in collisions and affect the navigation decisions of the attacked vessel. Another relatively vulnerable system is the electronic chart display and information system (ECDIS). The ECDIS is the computer-based navigation system of a vessel. It is connected to the Internet as well as to the standard communication platforms. According to Belmont, hacking the ECDIS may have severe consequences as it can alter charts as well as download, delete, and replace data. Unlike the AIS, the ECDIS is more susceptible to attack due to the potential human error or negligence.[8] This is because most charts are updated via USB keys, which are directly connected to the computer and allow the information to be uploaded. Even though it is almost impossible to be fully protected, USB keys are scanned for malware on a separate computer, which does not contain any sensible or vital systems and is completely independent to the rest of the vessel's systems.

Regardless of the above-noted concerns and dangers, the maritime route remains the most efficient and cost effective. A single vessel can transfer significantly more cargo in a single trip than any other means of transport.

The second most prevalent route is the Southern land route, starting in Eastern China, most probably Beijing. The next connection will possibly be Xian, which is of great historical importance because it once was considered a center within the ancient Silk Road network. From there, cargo will travel through various Chinese cities via rail and trucks, where it will be arriving at the CPEC or Urumqi. Taking the second alternative to Urumqi, the next stop would be Kazakhstan followed by Turkmenistan, Iran, and finally Turkey. While considering the first option, through CPEC, the cargo may continue toward either Afghanistan or Iran directly, also ending up in Turkey for redistribution within the Balkans and the rest of Europe.

The most important advantage of the Southern route is clearly depicted in this scenario. When choosing a transfer of goods, companies will have the option to combine two of the OBOR initiative's routes. This will potentially minimize expenses and, therefore, maximize a company's earnings. Something China must take into consideration, though, when considering this route is politics. By choosing this route, the starting and ending points of the main journey are clear, China and Turkey, respectively.

The two countries could potentially be making commercial decisions excluding Russia's interests. Completely excluding Russia and therefore all members of the EAEU might prove detrimental to the OBOR initiative. This, however, is an unlikely scenario as the leaders of the two countries have created strong diplomatic bonds.[9] Moreover, in July 2017, China Development Bank and the Russian Direct Investment Fund signed the China–Russia RMB Investment Cooperation Fund. The investments will total $10 billion[10] and will include OBOR initiative projects. Nonetheless, China is bypassing Russia to some extent by negotiating with EAEU members individually,[11] thus creating some uncertainty on how future events will unfold.

The third and final route being considered by the Chinese is the Northern route. In this mapping, travels commence in Beijing and possibly pass through Xian, similar to the Southern route. However, the trip would continue through Mongolia and Siberia, ending in Moscow. Although incorporating Russia, this route poses two major disadvantages for the Chinese. First, the weather conditions are harsh and any development in the area requires more time and money. Second, China will have very little control over goods during most of the journey because the majority of the passage occurs on Russian territory. To make sure, however, that all interests are served and that none of the major players are excluded a combination of the routes most likely will be utilized on a daily basis. Decisions on routes will probably be made based upon the nature of the cargo being transported and the commercial requirements of the cargo owners.

Despite the general notion of inclusion, the Chinese have made clear that not all are welcomed to participate in the initiative. Japan, for example, is not included in any of the possible routes and is not considered as an ally in this project. Even though Japan is China's number one trading partner in imports,[12] Japan does not depend upon China. Moreover, due to the long-lasting and ongoing trade war between the two countries, even if Japan is included in the OBOR initiative its role may be limited. Despite all this, in 2017, Japan voiced its support for the project, as it helps multinational companies to expand in other countries.[13] Although not against and partly included in the initiative, Japan is promoting its own *Free and Open Indo-Pacific Strategy* (FOIP). The main aim of FOIP is that all countries supporting Japan's views will be assisted by it in order to create stability and profits in the region. This strategic coalition provides support to countries for the upcoming global changes, including the OBOR initiative[14]

Irrespective of Japan's support and its FOIP coalition, the OBOR initiative appears to be well established and dominating the Indo-Pacific area. Moreover, it appears that China will include some countries in the initiative, in multiple routes, for political and other reasons irrespective of cargo considerations. Candidate countries must be situated in a key geographical location and provide both land and sea access. One such nation that squares away all such requirements, including a strategically significant geography and trade history, is Greece and more specifically its Piraeus port.

NOTES

1 "Belt and Road Initiative." *Belt and Road Initiative.* Last modified April 29, 2018. www.beltroad-initiative.com/belt-and-road/.

2 Tafero, Paul E., and Arthur Tafero. *China Strategies in the Belt and Road Initiative.* Independently Published, 2019. https://www.bookdepository.com/China-Strategies-Belt-Road-Initiative-Paul-Eberle-Dr-Arthur-Tafero/9781095227565.

3 "Three Factors That Have Made Singapore a Global Logistics Hub." *World Bank Blogs.* Last modified November 7, 2019. https://blogs.worldbank.org/transport/three-factors-have-made-singapore-global-logistics-hub.

4 "Three Factors That Have Made Singapore a Global Logistics Hub." *World Bank Blogs.* Last modified November 7, 2019. https://blogs.worldbank.org/transport/three-factors-have-made-singapore-global-logistics-hub.

5 "Construction Starts at Damerjog LNG Terminal in Djibouti." *World Maritime News.* Last modified March 3, 2016. https://worldmaritimenews.com/archives/184628/construction-starts-at-damerjog-lng-terminal-in-djibouti/.

6 "International Maritime Bureau." *ICC: Commercial Crime Services.* Last modified July 7, 2017. www.icc-ccs.org/icc/imb.

7 Gontika, Tatiana. *Defining Maritime Cyber Terrorism.* Bronx, NY: SUNY Maritime College, 2019. Paper submitted as a term paper in TMGT 8499 Maritime Physical, Operational & Cyber Security.

8 Direnzo, Joseph, III, et al. *Issues in Maritime Cyber Security.* Washington, DC: Westphalia Press, 2017.

9 Ming, Cheang. "'Best Time in History' for China-Russia Relationship: Xi and Putin Boost Ties." *CNBC.* Last modified July 5, 2017. www.cnbc.com/2017/07/04/china-russia-ties-reaffirmed-after-xi-jinping-and-vladimir-putin-meet.html.

10 Xiao, Cai. "China, Russia Set Up RMB Investment Fund." *Global Edition.* Last modified July 5, 2017. www.chinadaily.com.cn/business/2017-07/05/content_30002107.htm.

11 Baumgartner, Pete. "China's Massive 'One Road' Project Largely Bypasses Russia, But Moscow Still on Board." *RadioFreeEurope/RadioLiberty.* Last modified June 26, 2017. www.rferl.org/a/russia-china-one-belt-one-road-project-putin-xi/28579849.html.

12 Tafero, Paul E., and Arthur Tafero. *China Strategies in the Belt and Road Initiative.* Independently Published, 2019. https://www.bookdepository.com/China-Strategies-Belt-Road-Initiative-Paul-Eberle-Dr-Arthur-Tafero/9781095227565.

13 Jennings, Ralph. "Japan Is Committing to China's Belt & Road Initiative, But What's in It for Them?" *Forbes.* Last modified April 17, 2018. www.forbes.com/sites/ralphjennings/2018/04/17/why-japan-had-to-join-china-in-building-trade-routes-around-asia/#5f531cd37175.

14 Mehta, Simi. "The Free and Open Indo-Pacific Strategy: A Way Forward." *Policy Forum.* Last modified July 25, 2019. www.policyforum.net/the-free-and-open-indo-pacific-strategy-a-way-forward/.

Chapter 7

Greece's Historical Overview

A detailed examination of Greece's ancient or modern history is of neither significant interest nor value for this paper. However, specific historical and political events that are relevant to grasp the contemporary situation in Greece merit discussion. Namely, during WWII Greece was occupied by the Germans. Severe damages, like those at the Piraeus port, were experienced all over Greece and numerous Greeks lost their lives. Children in some rural areas, like my grandfather,[1] would strike deals with the German soldiers trading pigeons they would catch for bread or other goods. On the other hand, in areas nearby, children, like my grandmother,[2] were terrified of the German soldiers because they had killed over half of the village's population. Overall, the Germans were the harshest occupiers the country suffered. Unfortunately, when the war ended, the exiled government returned to find a divided country, the outcome of which would be a devastating civil war.

The first stage of the *Greek Civil War* (GCW) began before the country's liberation. In addition to fighting the Nazi occupiers and the Axis powers, Greek resistance would be fighting amongst themselves. The resistance was divided into two groups: the National Liberation Front, *Εθνικό Απελευθερωτικό Μέτωπο* (EAM) along with its paramilitary units the Greek Liberation Army, *Ελληνικός Απελευθερωτικός Στρατός* (ELAS), and the National Republican Greek League *Εθνικός Δημοκρατικός Ελληνικός Σύνδεσμος* (EDES). During the last months of WWII, the communist resistance forces EAM and ELAS would launch terror campaigns against their opponents, both Greeks and non-Greeks.

In December 1944, only a few months after the country's liberation, the second phase of the GCW would commence. The December events, commonly referred to as the Dekemvriana (*Δεκεμβριανά*), marked one of the worst periods in the nation's history. The unrest started in Athens, on December 3, 1944, during a pro-EAM rally in the city center.

The main motive for the rally was that EAM ministers, who were initially part of the government, had resigned due to unresolvable differences with the British-backed government. Unable to handle the rally, and in an attempt to shut it down, police forces killed 28 protesters and wounded 148.[3] This initial incident resulted in further killings and an armed confrontation between the EAM forces and the National Army, led by the British General, Ronald Scoble. The Dekemvriana officially ended in February 1945 with the signing of the Treaty of Varkiza.[4] After the peace treaty was signed, EAM was neutralized, making individuals affiliated with the communist party an easy target.

In the months that followed, a terror campaign was initiated against all known or assumed supporters of the communist party. The government backed *White Terror* period actions, leading to the imprisonment and execution of many.

Some of the EAM/ELAS members fled to the mountains and engaged in guerilla warfare. In December 1946, the remaining supporters of EAM realigned themselves with the Greek Democratic Army, *Δημοκρατικός Στρατός Ελλάδας* (DSE). Greece's communist party, the Κομμουνιστικό Κόμμα Ελλάδας (KKE), fully controlled the DSE and deployed it to assist the upcoming communist regimes in the Balkans. This proved to be the communists' fatal mistake. Their success was based on their guerilla style, unpredictable attacks as well as their manpower; therefore, the usual symmetric battlefield strategy was detrimental. Another aspect that changed and eventually led to the DSE's defeat was the negative shift of public opinion. The significant shift was caused because of the abduction of almost 30,000 children, who were sent to Balkan countries to be trained and become members of the communist military force.

Finally, the KKE was defeated because of its open support of Stalin's regime. One of KKE's main supporters, ally and source of help was Yugoslavia under dictator Josip Broz Tito. Stalin and Tito had various conflicts, which eventually led to Yugoslavia's expulsion from the Communist Information Bureau in 1948. Therefore, by supporting Stalin's regime, the KKE was supporting the enemy in the eyes of Yugoslavia. Without Tito's support, the DSE lost their military training base and instructors as well as their principal supplier. After the official defeat of the DSE, on October 16, 1948, many fled the country and others were imprisoned.

Greece remained politically divided and its economy was severely damaged, leaving the nation largely dependent upon the US aid.

Greece's future would not be brighter in the years to follow. In 1950 alone, characterized by political instability, Greece went through six prime ministers. In 1952, Alexandros Papagos, a GCW commander, became prime minister. Papagos' government freed many non-political prisoners but executed those convicted for political crimes. Although many of his actions are questionable and unethical, living standards improved dramatically during his regime.

Many Greeks who had fled the country started to return and establish new businesses with the money they had earned abroad. Moreover, the Greek marine industry emerged as the largest in the world upon the purchase of surplus US Liberty ships built during WWII.[5]

After the death of Papagos and in the middle of the Cypriot crisis, Konstantinos Karamanlis won the 1956 elections becoming the youngest prime minister in the nation's history. Karamanlis supported the Americans and the aid they were providing, for which he was greatly criticized. According to some, it was during his government that extreme right supporters started establishing groups that persecuted left wing supporters. Karamanlis, however, was successful in rebuilding the Greek economy. During the following decade, governments changed and the Greek economy stabilized. However, the country's political, and therefore national, division did not heal.

On April 21, 1967, another sad part of Greece's history commenced, when a coup forced a military government, Χούντα,[6] on the nation. Colonels Papadopoulos, Patakos, and Makarezos led the coup, whose alleged purpose was to save Greece from the communist threat. During this dark period, many were killed, disappeared, or became exiled. Papadopoulos became the country's dictator in December 1967. He forbade free speech, strikes, as well as large gatherings, excluding those in churches. Moreover, he attempted to rewrite the textbooks taught in higher education as well as control the history taught to students. The regime was so conservative that many writers, such as Shakespeare and Aristophanes, were banned. They also banned long hair for men and miniskirts for women. In May 1973, Papadopoulos declared Greece a republic and declared himself its president. On November 17 of the same year, tanks invaded the National Technical University of Athens killing over 30 students.[7] This event marked the beginning of the end of the dictatorship.

It took over half a year for the country to enter the new era known as *Μεταπολίτευση* (Metapoliteusi).[8] On July 24, 1974, the first elections of Greece's modern history took place and Konstantinos Karamanlis became Prime Minister again. This period consists of the four decades from the restoration of democracy until the 2009 elections and the commencement of the economic crisis. One of the most significant events of this period was the legalization of KKE and other leftist parties as well as the establishment of the new Greek constitution, which remains in effect today with minor amendments. Moreover, irrespective of party allegiance, subsequent leaders tried to bridge the political and national division that had started during WWII.

It was during the period of Metapoliteusi in which Greece's two major parties were founded. On the one hand, Andreas Papandreou, who had been politically active prior to the dictatorship, created the center-left party called *Panhellenic Socialist Movement* (PASOK), on September 3, 1974. On the other hand, the country's leader, Konstantinos Karamanlis established the center-right party called *New Democracy* (ND), on October 4, 1974. In total, through his political career, Konstantinos Karamanlis would win six elections and Andreas Papandreou three. The two parties combined have won 18 of the 24 elections since 1974.

During his first term as Prime Minister, Andreas Papandreou focused on minimizing social inequalities as well as the establishment and reinforcement of the middle class. Additionally, in his first term, an effort was made for the country to comply with various regulations of the European Community, which it had joined in 1981. Although not yet financially stable, Greece was attracting both foreign and domestic investors. Another major issue of the time was the relations between Greece and Turkey, which had been fractured following the Turkish invasion of Cyprus in 1974.

In the decades to follow, one of the most well-respected political leaders was Konstantinos Mitsotakis, who won the 1993 elections. The Mitsotakis family was one of the families that had fled to Paris during the Papadopoulos dictatorship. One of his government's first actions was to minimize public expenses. Additionally, efforts were made to privatize state enterprises and reform civil service. The opposition challenged and heavily criticized these policies. The opposition also criticized Mitsotakis's foreign policy, especially the recognition of the State of Israel.

Moreover, as relations between Greece and the United States had suffered under the preceding Papandreou government, Mitsotakis attempted

to bridge the gap between the two nations. He guaranteed Greece's com-
pliance with NATO's obligations under the auspices of thwarting a potential terrorist base.

The aforementioned actions were not the basis of the primary criticism directed at him. Rather, the opposition and members of ND accused
Mitsotakis of leniency on the naming of the newly independent Republic
of Macedonia. The naming of the country is an issue which is discussed
until today and has become one of Greece's major issues of foreign affairs.
The issue dates back to the 1980s but really escalated in 1991 when the
country was declared an independent state in need of a new name and
flag.[9] On the one hand, the Greek side has been arguing that the name
Macedonia should only be used for the northern part of Greece. The area
was home to Alexander the Great who similarly to his predecessors used
the Sun of Vergina (*Το Αστέρι της Βεργίνας*) as their symbol. On the other
hand, due to its geographical location, which is indeed part of the ancient
Macedonian kingdom the country was named Former Yugoslav Republic
of Macedonia (FYROM) and depicted the Sun of Vergina in their flag. The
dispute on the flag was solved and the North Macedonia state changing its
flag. The name dispute on the other hand was not solved until 2018, where
the two sides finally came to an agreement.[10]

One of the longest active Greek Prime Ministers was Konstantinos
Simitis who was in office for over eight years. He sought, through his policies, to modernize Greece's socialist government. Simitis was similar to
Mitsotakis, though more moderate, he promoted privatization, such as the
successful move to the private sector of the Hellenic Telecommunications
Organization (OTE). OTE was founded in October 1949 and launched
that same year. Within 30 years of operations, OTE provided national
and international coverage, and in 1989, the first fully digital telephone
exchange operated in Patras.[11] Another milestone year was 1999, where
mobile telecommunications networks offered 97% population coverage.[12]
That same decade OTE expanded to the Balkans, acquiring stakes in
RomTelecom and GSM License in Romania and Bulgaria, respectively. The
Greek state started selling the company's stocks to institutional investors
in late 2000s and finally reached an agreement with Deutsche Telekom,
who by 2018 owned 45% of OTE's shares.[13]

Furthermore, in his second term, Simitis implemented austerity measures, reducing both the country's inflation and national debt, resulting,
in 2001, in Greece's entry into the eurozone. He also tried to improve relations with neighboring Turkey.

In the elections of May 2004, ND's leader Konstantinos A. Karamanlis (Prime Minister Karamanlis) won the elections. Thirty years after the reestablishment of democracy, the Karamanlis government was receiving the country in a fairly stable condition. Upon his election, Prime Minister Karamanlis's major concern was to restructure the country's economy. All of the government's new policies were criticized by the masses, who organized protest and, in some cases, strikes. In his first term, Karamanlis accomplished his goal as the country's economy improved in the next years.

In September 2007, Prime Minister Karamanlis won his second term but two years later lost to George Papandreou, the leader of PASOK. At the time, many of his supporters were dismayed and criticized Prime Minister Karamanlis for calling early elections in the heart of the global economic crisis.

Soon after being sworn in, the new Prime Minister Papandreou revealed to the Greek people that the previous government's borrowing and its budget deficit were far worse than reported. The Greek economy, previously stable under Simitis and Karamanlis, suddenly became severely disrupted because of governmental overspending and mismanagement. Papandreou in an attempt to improve the country's economy tried implementing austerity measures. These measures were unpopular with the Greek people who strongly protested. It was not until 2010, however, that the actual amount of the Greek debt was made public knowledge and the country asked for its first, of three, internationally sourced bailouts. Since then, Greece has received 289 billion Euros ($330 billion) and has been urged, by the European Commission, European Central Bank, and the IMF (the Troika), to take further and harsher austerity measures.

One of these measures, which has been heavily discussed by those affected as well as their families, was that of pension reforms, which both increased the age of retirement and reduced the amount paid. In addition to decreased pensions, tax increases severely affected Greek households and businesses particularly since, in both public and private sectors, employees saw their wages cut and, in some cases, even frozen.

Within five years of the implementation of Papandreou's reforms, Greeks became on average 40% poorer, and because of the almost nonexistent social welfare system, more than a third of the country experienced severe material deprivation.[14] One of the first things most Greeks believe that a government should improve and the last it should jeopardize is the country's healthcare system. However, during the past few years, healthcare has been one of the hardest hit sectors in Greece.

Hospitals are lacking not only doctors and nurses but also medicine and basic supplies like bandages,[15] a situation that clearly depicts the dramatically decreasing quality of life of Greek citizens. Moreover, due to these austerity measures, the availability of mental healthcare services has declined at a time when the nation needs it the most. The increased number of suicides[16] is one of the many examples of how desperate Greeks are becoming.

The overall situation in Greece along with other measures taken over the years has led to what economists refer to as "brain drain." Most young Greeks have left their home country or have not returned after studying abroad, as job opportunities are scarce. According to BBC's Lucy Rodgers and Nassos Stylianou, a quarter of Greece's population was unemployed in 2015, out of which half were under 25 years of age. Fortunately, since the beginning of 2017, this phenomenon has somewhat halted and some of the young educated expatriates are returning. Of course, the options for them remain tenuous as the average monthly salary is around €700, nonetheless some are choosing to remain. Regardless of some signs of the economy's improvement, 45% of Greeks under 25 years of age remain unemployed. Moreover, teenagers graduating high school still consider studying and working abroad as the best option for their future. This option is, of course, quite detrimental for the future of the nation.[17]

Thus, Greece suffers not only economically but socially as well. The ancient and once united country is now divided while the overall safety in the nation's capital, Athens, is questionable. In the 2015 elections, the anti-austerity party, the Coalition of Radical Left, Συνασπισμός Ριζοσπαστικής Αριστεράς (SYRIZA), led by Alexis Tsipras, won the elections receiving almost 75% of the votes after promising various changes, such as increases in salaries and pensions. Such promises contradicted the IMF's requirements for bailout and created hostility between European nations, such as Germany and Greece. Simultaneously, however, left-wing leaders from around the world saw the Greek election results as a victory and beginning of a new era for Europe. Pablo Iglesias, leader of Spain's far-left Podemos, and Pierre Laurent, secretary-general of France's Communist Party, were both present in SYRIZA's final campaign rally.

Only a few months after the elections and upon unsuccessful aggressive negotiations with the IMF, in July 2015, Prime Minister Tsipras called for

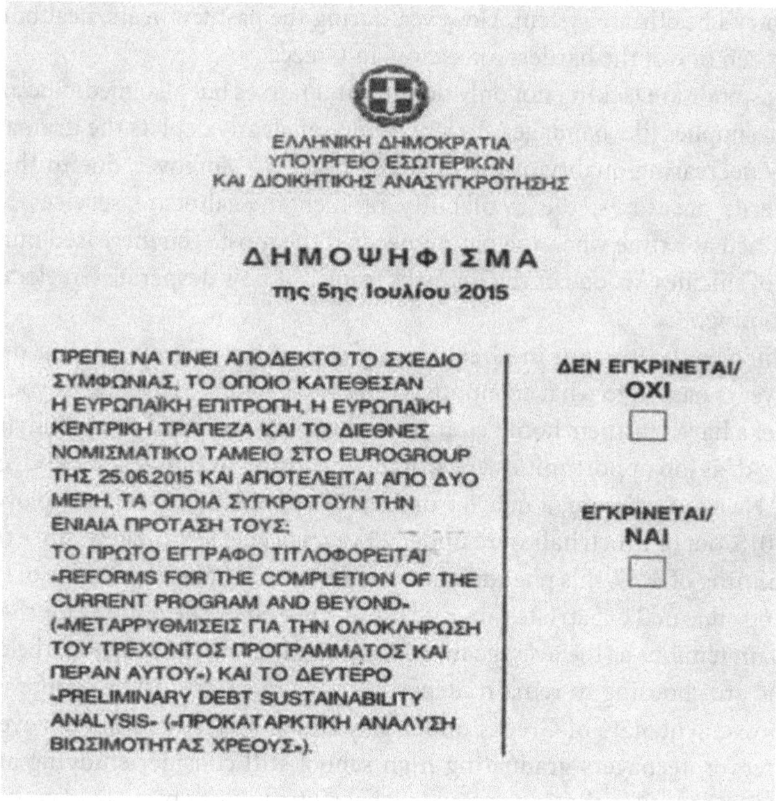
ΕΛΛΗΝΙΚΗ ΔΗΜΟΚΡΑΤΙΑ
ΥΠΟΥΡΓΕΙΟ ΕΣΩΤΕΡΙΚΩΝ
ΚΑΙ ΔΙΟΙΚΗΤΙΚΗΣ ΑΝΑΣΥΓΚΡΟΤΗΣΗΣ

ΔΗΜΟΨΗΦΙΣΜΑ
της 5ης Ιουλίου 2015

ΠΡΕΠΕΙ ΝΑ ΓΙΝΕΙ ΑΠΟΔΕΚΤΟ ΤΟ ΣΧΕΔΙΟ ΣΥΜΦΩΝΙΑΣ, ΤΟ ΟΠΟΙΟ ΚΑΤΕΘΕΣΑΝ Η ΕΥΡΩΠΑΪΚΗ ΕΠΙΤΡΟΠΗ, Η ΕΥΡΩΠΑΪΚΗ ΚΕΝΤΡΙΚΗ ΤΡΑΠΕΖΑ ΚΑΙ ΤΟ ΔΙΕΘΝΕΣ ΝΟΜΙΣΜΑΤΙΚΟ ΤΑΜΕΙΟ ΣΤΟ EUROGROUP ΤΗΣ 25.06.2015 ΚΑΙ ΑΠΟΤΕΛΕΙΤΑΙ ΑΠΟ ΔΥΟ ΜΕΡΗ, ΤΑ ΟΠΟΙΑ ΣΥΓΚΡΟΤΟΥΝ ΤΗΝ ΕΝΙΑΙΑ ΠΡΟΤΑΣΗ ΤΟΥΣ:
ΤΟ ΠΡΩΤΟ ΕΓΓΡΑΦΟ ΤΙΤΛΟΦΟΡΕΙΤΑΙ «REFORMS FOR THE COMPLETION OF THE CURRENT PROGRAM AND BEYOND» («ΜΕΤΑΡΡΥΘΜΙΣΕΙΣ ΓΙΑ ΤΗΝ ΟΛΟΚΛΗΡΩΣΗ ΤΟΥ ΤΡΕΧΟΝΤΟΣ ΠΡΟΓΡΑΜΜΑΤΟΣ ΚΑΙ ΠΕΡΑΝ ΑΥΤΟΥ») ΚΑΙ ΤΟ ΔΕΥΤΕΡΟ «PRELIMINARY DEBT SUSTAINABILITY ANALYSIS» («ΠΡΟΚΑΤΑΡΚΤΙΚΗ ΑΝΑΛΥΣΗ ΒΙΩΣΙΜΟΤΗΤΑΣ ΧΡΕΟΥΣ»).

ΔΕΝ ΕΓΚΡΙΝΕΤΑΙ/
ΟΧΙ

ΕΓΚΡΙΝΕΤΑΙ/
ΝΑΙ

FIGURE 7.1
Referendum (July 5, 2015).

a referendum, further dividing the already hurt society (see Figure 7.1).[18] In late June 2015, Tsipras asked the people of Greece to vote whether his government should enforce more budget cuts in exchange for a financial aid package. In the actual referendum, there is no reference as to the country's future in the eurozone. However, it was made clear by the troika that failure to fulfill their requirements by their deadline would mean exactly that.[19] During the pre-referendum days, Tsipras campaigned against the bailout and urged the people to vote "no." On July 5, 2015, 61% voted "no" instructing the government not to sign the new bailout agreement and essentially agreeing to a GREXIT.[20] Tsipras imposed capital controls hours after the referendum and Greeks found themselves queuing to withdraw money from the ATMs. Additionally, to the capital controls, a week later Tsipras did, indeed, signed the same measures he had fought against.

More than three years later, the society, unable to heal, remains wounded; there are cases, especially in the smaller islands and villages, where families fought amongst themselves and to this day have not reunited. However, what has altered is the citizens approval and satisfaction with the leading party and their Prime Minister. One of the main reasons Tsipras won both the January and September 2015 elections was because of his vow to change practical matters that would directly affect the everyday lives of the suffering Greeks, that is, improve living conditions and terminating the prior government's efforts to privatize all facets of Greek society.

After almost four years in power, Prime Minister Tsipras's government became highly criticized by both its original supporters and the opposition. After losing the May 2019 European Parliament elections, Tsipras immediately called for new Greek parliamentary elections, which he lost.

In July 2019, Kyriakos Mitsotakis became Prime Minister of Greece. His win is perceived by many as Greece's chance to get out of the long, seemingly unending crisis that began in 2009 with Papandreou's revelations about Greece's fiscal instability. Moreover, the government is constantly trying to improve the country's position in the international markets and at the same time attract more investments. Finally, unlike the previous government, the current government is supporting various foreign investment including COSCO's in Piraeus.

NOTES

1 My maternal grandfather was born in Tripoli a village in the middle of the Peloponnese (1931–2010).
2 My paternal grandmother was born outside Kalavryta, a mountainous village in the North of the Peloponnese (1936–2019).
3 GCT. "Dekemvriana, One of the Saddest Days in Greece's History." *Greek City Times*. Last modified December 6, 2019. https://greekcitytimes.com/2018/12/03/commemorating-dekemvriana-when-first-shots-are-fired-in-athens/.
4 *Foreign Relations of the United States: Diplomatic Papers, 1945: The Near East and Africa, Volume VIII*. 1945. https://history.state.gov/historicaldocuments/frus1945v08/d63.
5 "History of Greece: Post-War." *History of Greece*. Last modified December 6, 2019. www.ahistoryofgreece.com/post-war.htm.
6 The years of the military dictatorship are referred to as Jounta.
7 Encyclopedia Britannica. "Giorgios Papadopoulos." n.d. Last modified December 6, 2019. www.britannica.com/biography/Giorgios-Papadopoulos.

8   Metapoliteusi is the period after the fall of the military junta and democracy was restored. This period ends with the 2009 elections and the economic crisis.

9   European Stability Initiative. "Macedonia's Dispute with Greece: Macedonia." *European Stability Initiative: ESI*. Last modified November 2012. www.esiweb.org/index.php?lang=en&id=562.

10 "Macedonia and Greece: Vote Settles 27-Year Name Dispute." *BBC News*. Last modified January 25, 2019. www.bbc.com/news/world-europe-47002865.

11 Patras is the third largest city of Greece, located in the norther Peloponnese is home to one of the busiest Greek ports.

12 "Timeline." *OTE*. Last modified December 3, 2019. www.cosmote.gr/cs/otegroup/en/otegroup_timeline.html.

13 Deutsche Telekom AG. "Deutsche Telekom Raises Stake in OTE's Share Capital by 5 Percent." *Deutsche Telekom: Deutsche Telekom*. Last modified May 30, 2018. www.telekom.com/en/media/media-information/archive/deutsche-telekom-raises-stake-in-ote-s-share-capital-by-5-percent-526212.

14 Rodgers, L., and N. Stylianou. *How Bad Are Things for the People of Greece?* July 16, 2015. Last modified November 9, 2018. www.bbc.com/news/world-europe-33507802.

15 Smith, Helena. "'Patients Who Should Live Are Dying': Greece's Public Health Meltdown." *The Guardian*. Last modified November 28, 2017. www.theguardian.com/world/2017/jan/01/patients-dying-greece-public-health-meltdown.

16 Kitsantonis, Niki. "Greece, 10 Years into Economic Crisis, Counts the Cost to Mental Health." *The New York Times: Breaking News, World News & Multimedia*. Last modified February 3, 2019. www.nytimes.com/2019/02/03/world/europe/greece-economy-mental-health.html.

17 All Quantitative information of this paragraph can be found: Rodgers, Lucy, and Nassos Stylianou. "How Bad Are Things for the Greeks?" *BBC News*. Last modified July 16, 2015. www.bbc.com/news/world-europe-33507802.

18 Illustration 7.1 from: "ΔΗΜΟΨΗΦΙΣΜΑ της 5ης Ιουλίου 2015." *Υπουργείο Εσωτερικών*. n.d. www.ypes.gr/UserFiles/f0ff9297-f516-40ff-a70e-eca84e2ec9b9/psfd-referendumB.jpg.

19 "Voters Don't Understand the Question." *The National Herald*. Last modified July 4, 2015. www.thenationalherald.com/90180/?utm_source=feedburner&utm_medium=feed&utm_campaign=Feed%3A+TNHTopStories+%28The+National+Herald+top+stories%29.

20 Abbreviation for "Greek Exit" refers to Greece's exit from the eurozone.

Chapter 8

Piraeus Port

Thucydides wrote that Piraeus was the port where *"from all the lands, everything enters."*[1] The port of Piraeus, consisting of three main harbors, Zea, Kantharos, and Munichia, has always been of great importance and a point of reference for traders all over the world. Located about 15 km away from Athens, Piraeus was always influenced by Athenians but also targeted by their enemies. The first, but not last, historical evidence of this was during the Peloponnese war in 431–404 BC. Although the area and the port were severely damaged, they were rebuilt and reestablished, as was the Athenian Democracy, which had also greatly suffered during the Peloponnese war. From then on, the port was reconstructed several times during the pre-Christian era.

Piraeus's first major period of inactivity occurred before the rise of the Byzantine empire when in AD 86, Piraeus was destroyed by the Roman general Sulla.[2] Additionally, once Constantinople was established as the Eastern Empire's capital, its port became the center of all commercial activities, and merchants lost their interest in Piraeus and the once safe port became a pirate hub.

After the fall of Constantinople to Mehmed II in 1453, Greece entered a long period of Turkish occupation. For almost 400 years, the port could not recover its previous status. Although pirate activity in the area eventually decreased, the port was only occasionally used. Visitors at the time agreed that Piraeus was a deserted place.[3] The years of the Ottoman occupation were tough for Piraeus and all over Greece, escalating in 1821 when Greece declared independence from the Ottomans and continuing during the ensuing nine years (1821–1830) of war between the Turks and the Greeks. In 1830, with the end of the war, a new era began for Piraeus, as well as the nation. As democracy was being rebuilt throughout the country, municipalities were being reestablished. The Piraeus municipality was established within four years, and in 1835, the first elections took place; Hydriot Kyriakos Serifotis was sworn as its first mayor.[4] The once abandoned area near Athens started to rise again.

One of the most important elements for Piraeus's rise was the variety of people moving there. Individuals and families from all over Greece were choosing Piraeus as a place of resettlement after the war. This created a well-rounded society and it rapidly started growing.[5] Moreover, in 1834, Athens became the country's capital, attracting even more residents to the nearby coastal city of Piraeus. During the 1840s, the port was perceived by merchants and travelers a "free port," and the first Greek-owned cargo vessel arrived. Finally, in 1869, the railroad connecting Athens to Piraeus was inaugurated. By the end of the 19th century, Piraeus had become the second city in Greece and the port found its lost glory. It took Greece many years to recover from the Ottoman occupation but as this was happening, Piraeus became Greece's leading port.

The first decades of the 20th century were fundamental for the development of the port and the city. It was then that Piraeus' first outer piers were constructed. Maritime traffic increased and the Greek government responded by establishing new measures to manage both imports and exports. The port gained managerial autonomy for the first time in its modern history when the Port Committee was established in 1911. Unfortunately, the Committee failed to successfully manage the port's operational needs, resulting in a revamping of the Committee through the establishment in 1930 of the Port of Piraeus Authority (PPA).

One of the PPA's main functions was managing the daily loading and discharge operations. To do so, it was given full autonomy and used its own labor force. Moreover, the PPA was authorized to charge both passenger and cargo vessels for any services provided. During that period of management by the PPA, the port's layout changed several times, including the installation in 1932 of its first cranes. Toward the end of the 1930s, various construction projects were completed, including the installation of additional technical equipment in port facilities.

The outbreak of World War II swiftly impacted the development and commercial use of the port. During the first months of the war, the Allies, primarily the British, utilized Piraeus port facilities. On April 6, 1941, the Germans began their occupation of Greece and a bombing campaign began. The campaign continued until the early morning of April 7. There have been various testimonies, including stories told to me by my grandparents, describing the horror of that night.

The first sirens sounded a few hours after sunset announcing the first German aircraft that flew over the area. People did not immediately believe that the airplane was a threat; it was thought that it was just mapping the port and surrounding area. However, a few hours later, the sirens sounded again and this time the alarm was real. Within hours, the whole area of Piraeus, including the port, was nearly destroyed. The destruction was such that it took the PPA five years to fully restore the facilities once Greece became independent again.

The 1950s and the 1960s were decisive, as the port started to become what it is today. Various projects were implemented targeting the port's further development and modernization. Two new warehouses were built, supervised by the Ministry of Merchant Marine.

During the *Χούντα* (the far-right dictatorship), the PPA was disassembled. The dictatorship lasted seven years, and it took 13 years after the fall of the dictatorship[6] before a new container terminal was built in Piraeus, an investment in 1987 worth 9.5 billion drachmas.[7]

A milestone year for the Piraeus Port was 1999, during which a vote by the Greek parliament converted the port facilities to a limited liability company; the PPA was also reestablished, funded by its own resources as well as by the European Investment Bank and the Cohesion Fund of the European Union.

Of course, the development of the Piraeus area and port is closely connected to the great Greek shipping tradition.

NOTES

1 Ebrahimi, Helia. "The Big Fat Greek Sell-Off." *Telegraph.co.uk*. Last modified June 5, 2011. www.telegraph.co.uk/finance/financialcrisis/8556698/The-big-fat-Greek-sell-off.html.
2 Catwright, Mark. "Piraeus." In *Ancient History Encyclopedia*. 2013. Last modified December 3, 2019. www.ancient.eu/Piraeus/.
3 Hadjimanolakis, Yannis E. "The Port of Piraeus through the Ages." *Home: Hellenic Electronic Center*. Last modified December 3, 2019. www.greece.org/poseidon/work/sea-ports/piraeus.html.
4 "Piraeus." *The Maritime Heritage Projects: Ships, Captains, Merchants, Passengers to 1800s San Francisco*. Last modified 2017. www.maritimeheritage.org/ports/greece Piraeus.
5 Hadjimanolakis, Yannis E. "The Port of Piraeus through the Ages." *Home: Hellenic Electronic Center*. Last modified December 3, 2019. www.greece.org/poseidon/work/sea-ports/piraeus.html.

6 Military dictatorship fell 1974, new container terminal built 1987. Thus, 13 years later.

7 "Chronology." *Piraeus Port Authority S.A.* Last modified December 6, 2019. www.olp.gr/en/the-port-of-piraeus/chronology.

Chapter 9

Greek Shipping

Merchants of various nations, actively including Greek merchants, have always exploited both the Mediterranean and the Black Sea. But the Greek merchant presence extended and continues to extend far beyond the home region of Greece, having been documented in London, Marseille, Livorno, as well as other major European ports since the early 1820s.[1]

Nationally, the world knows Greece for its tradition in shipping, but there are certain locations within Greece, mostly islands, that have a much longer history and presence in the shipping tradition than the nation as a whole. The oldest example of such an island is Chios (see Figure 9.1), located only 46.8 nautical miles (86.70 km) from Izmir, Turkey.[2]

The island's organized shipping tradition is documented as early as the 1830s.[3] Many Chiots fled Greece and moved to England and other European countries, especially during the Greek revolution against the Turks. Their ties with their motherland and their presence in major European ports gave them a unique advantage over other traders. Their open line of communication and the Greek and European knowhow made them dominant in their fields. By 1860, 57% of all tonnage entering British ports from the eastern Mediterranean and the Black Sea was handled by Greek merchants.[4]

The Chiots mostly focused on bulk cargoes, such as grain and cotton, when sailing to north and northwestern Europe. On their return voyage to eastern Mediterranean ports, such as Constantinople, Alexandria, and so on, they carried manufactured goods, such as textiles and threads. In nearly all ports of call, Greek merchants developed special relations. In Alexandria, for example, Greek traders gradually, and due to the financial difficulties faced by Muhammad Ali's[5] government, bought most of the cotton harvest houses from the Egyptian state. In that way, they eliminated the intermediaries and maximized profit.

FIGURE 9.1
Map of Chios.

Another reason Greek merchants, and especially the Chiots, became dominant was the international and domestic importance of Syros (see Figure 9.2).[6] Since the establishment of the Greek state in 1830, Syros became the center of all Greek maritime activity, later to be replaced by Piraeus. The island's most important town Ermoupolis is, to this day, the capital of the Cyclades, in the Aegean Sea. In Syros, seamen were able to build, repair, or sell their ships and also insure and charter them. Most importantly, because of its location in the heart of the Aegean, the island was a passage and reference point, thus becoming a center of valuable market information.

Syros was financially dependent, to a large scale, on the Chiot traders. Not only were they handling most of the island's commerce but they also built almost all of their ships in the shipyards of Syros. In a time when most of the Greek-flag fleet was Chiot, it is estimated that over half of it was built in Syros.[7] Therefore, it was no surprise when the island started losing its significance once the Chiot network started to weaken.

FIGURE 9.2
Map of Syros.

In hindsight, the Chiot network was essential for Greece's establishment in the maritime world. The most important factor, continuing into
the present day, is that because of the Chiots, there developed a strong
Greek presence in London. Secondly, by uprooting to England, the
Chiots were able to establish a trading and shipping network throughout Europe, avoiding most intermediaries. Finally, they organized the
already existing trade and were able to provide new trading partners
for the Greek-flag fleet. Although considered one of the strongest and
well-established networks of its time, the Chiots were unable to maintain their position, mostly due to the Crimean War[8] as well as internal
factors, such as the replacement of the old generation by the new and
inexperienced. Therefore, their commercial activities dropped significantly during the 1860s. While the Chiot network was falling, the Ionian
network was on the rise and taking over.

The Ionian network consisted of merchants from mostly Kefalonia and Ithaca, both part of the *Επτάνησα* (the Seven Ionian Islands). Located between Greece and Italy, the Ionian Islands were close to the mainland and historically had suffered less from the Ottoman rule than those located in Eastern Greek waters. At the time of the Ionian uprising, steamships were rapidly replacing sailboats. Moreover, the outbreak of the Crimean War in 1853 severely affected the trading in the Black Sea area and shifted it toward the inland Danube. It was there where the Ionian presence was the strongest. Before the 1860s, almost half of the total tonnage left the Danube in Greek owned vessels.[9] This number, however, significantly dropped during the 1870s, 1880s until the 1890s due to the slow Greek transition from sails to steam. However, the Ionians bounced back, and by 1914, over 60% of the Greek steamships were owned or financed by them.[10]

The outbreak of WWI in 1914 indeed affected Greek shipping, but not in a counterproductive way, as some expected. During and due to the war, new routes were introduced and Greek shipowners took advantage of these opportunities. Additionally, the strong demand on ship transport generated unexpected profits. It was during this period that Greek shipping transitioned to transoceanic. Nearly half of the Greek fleet consisted of deep-water vessels able to perform such journeys and were chartered and exploited by the Allies. The charters, combined with the rocketing freight rates, collectively generated profits of around £8 million for shipowners.[11] Moreover, and as in all wars, many vessels were sunk or severely damaged, creating a shortage of readily available ships and therefore increasing market value. Many Greek owners saw this unique opportunity and sold their vessels.

As the war ended, Greece was financially hurt. In an effort to boost both its economy and the Greek fleet, the Greek government established a new law imposing taxes on "exceptional profits." Exceptional profits were defined as those made during the war, including but not limited to those earned by chartering, trading, or selling vessels. The first portion of the law related to the profits made due to a vessel's operation. The second taxed the difference of the selling of the vessel during the war and the vessel's original pre-war price. This second tax had an important footnote. If owners were to replace the vessel sold during the war, they would get that tax refunded. This resulted in the doubling of the Greek fleet in only four years after the war.[12] The government annulled the first part of the law, regarding profit taxation, and replaced it by 1918. The new law offered tax exemption on all profits generated by Greek-flag vessels.

In the years following WWI, Greek shipping routes would return to their pre-war course. The Greek fleet grew significantly, becoming the ninth largest in the world and established itself amongst the top in dry-cargo tramp fleets. The most astonishing characteristic of Greek shipping and shipowners at the time was the effect the global shipping crisis of the 1930s had on them. During that period, while other countries with long shipping tradition were suffering, the Greek fleet grew substantially. Greek owners started buying vessels not for replacements or specific trading deals but as investments. Essentially, Greek owners were buying cheap to sell for a significant profit.

That grace period, however, soon ended with the outbreak of WWII. The 1940s were a troubled decade for the world and Greece was no exception. In the early months of the war, Greek shipowners and the Greek state, who had once mutually benefited from each other, were at odds. The Greek state in an attempt to stop shipowners from profiting as they did during WWI established fixed rates for Greek-flag fleet chartering. This initiative was seen by the Greek owners as a sellout to foreign powers, which was inaccurate as their fleets were treated similar to other European fleets.

Such issues were not solved once WWII ended, largely due to the GCW. Therefore, many of the remaining ship owning families fled to London and New York. In an attempt to cut ties with Greece and in order to exploit benefits provided by other countries, large parts of the Greek fleet changed flag. As political stability was restored, the Greek government recognized the losses generated by the absence of shipping. In an attempt to lure shipowners back to Greece, the government took two main actions. First, it gave shipping companies liberal tax incentives, and second, the government committed to adopting non-interventionist policies.

Following the global economic trend, the shipping industry evolved significantly. The maritime trade, which in 1948 was estimated around 490 million tones, by the end of 1973 was over 3,000 million tones.[13] The shipping market during the postwar years was divided into two main categories: tankers and dry-cargo. This division contributed to the success of Greek shipowners. During the late 1940s and early 1950s, many Greeks invested in the tanker market. Aristotle Onassis and Stavros Niarchos are probably the most well-known example, who along with others took advantage of the increased demand in tanker vessels. It is because of them the term "*supertanker*" was established. When Onassis ordered the *Tina Onassis*, able to carry 45,000 dwt, approximately three times what tanker vessels were able to carry at the time[14] he revolutionized the Greek industry.

The increased demand in tankers led to the creation of legends such as Onassis. Moreover, it also created the perfect circumstances for a new period, that of the introduction of new shipowners who began to invest in the liquid-cargo market. The numbers of the Greek fleet rapidly grew, and by 1974, the Greek-owned tanker fleet accounted for 17% of the global fleet.[15] During the oil crises of 1973 and 1978, the Greek tanker fleet shrank by 38%,[16] but started growing again at the end of the 1980s and 1990s.

Generally, the rise of the Greek-owned fleet followed the international economic trends in the postwar years, but often appeared to be independent to the country's domestic economy, particularly because of the lack of taxation and governmental control that it enjoyed. Although many of the shipowners had headquarters in Piraeus, the vast majority of vessels were involved with foreign trade. As a result, a very small portion of shipping profits entered the country.

The Greek shipowners influenced the Greek economy in two main ways. They brought shipping capital or *shipping foreign exchange* into Greece primarily to cover the payments made directly to seamen and shipowners. Shipowners also used of their foreign capital to make investments. Through them, they establish their presence in other sectors of the country's economy. Greek shipowners have historically invested in various secondary and tertiary industries.

As per its definition, the secondary sector of the economy is the transformation of raw materials extracted to finished goods and consists of all manufacturing, processing, and construction jobs. Thus, Greek shipowners who have invested in the secondary economy have focused, among other things, on refining petroleum and coal, as well as mining non-metallic minerals. Moreover, those interested in the tertiary sector of the economy, also known as the service industry, have invested into banks, insurance companies as well as others.

It is important to highlight another major advantage that Greek shipowners held against the world. Most of them, especially the *"new-owners,"* purchased secondhand vessels to either create or expand their fleet. Onassis is only one such example, who purchased a U.S. Liberty ship and converted it according to his needs. The age of the vessels, which others would have considered a weakness, was used to their benefit. The companies operating them faced lower fixed costs and were therefore able to offer more competitive prices. During the late 1980s, however, this became one of the biggest disadvantages of the Greek-owned fleet. Due to various new regulations, especially those focusing on the environment, large portions of the fleet needed updating. This wave of modernization lasted for approximately two decades. In an attempt to comply, Greek shipowners started investing in new buildings or bought secondhand vessels when their prices dropped significantly during the late 1990s. According to data published by Murphy in 2011, the average age of vessels of in the Greek-owned fleet was 11 years old, almost two years younger than the rest of the world's fleet.[17]

The strength of the Greek-owned fleet is evident throughout its history. Irrespective of all global crises, it has managed to survive and, in some cases, become stronger through the crises. During the past decade, the Greek economy has been suffering, and even though the shipping sector has been affected, it still remains strong and is one of the driving industries of the nation. In 2015, it accounted for 4% of the country's GDP equal to $9 billion.[18] Shipping is one of the few Greek industries in which employees retain a sense of job security.

Shipping companies have primarily been unaffected by the national crisis because the nature of their business as international traders is that they do not rely exclusively upon the Greek economy. Many of the companies are based in convenience flag states such as Panama and Liberia, which are considered tax havens; only the managing companies are located in Piraeus or other locations in Greece. This has generated criticism from those uninvolved in the shipping industry.

A general feeling of division, economic disparity, and instability has led people to argue that the tax benefits as well as the power Greek shipowners have are some of Greece's main problems. This critique, however, is somewhat inaccurate, because early in the crisis generated by the 2008 economic meltdown, the shipowners paid voluntary contributions that, as of 2013, totaled €420 million additional taxes to the Greek government. The purpose was to help stabilize the country.[19]

In early 2019, the prime minister's office announced that the voluntary agreement between the Greek shipowners and the state, which had expired, had been replaced. According to the new agreement, shipowners were expected to pay at least €75 million annually to the state budget.[20]

The Greek shipping industry is a fundamental part of both the Greek economy and the world economy. According to the Union of Greek Shipowners (UGS), 98.5% of the trading of the Greek-owned fleet is among third countries and shifts according to global demand.[21] Moreover, due to the fleet's major trade partners, the EU and the United States, the country's profile and entrepreneurial identity is constantly improving irrespective of its economy. As stated in UGS's article *Greek Shipping and Economy 2018*, the numbers are impressive. Greek owners carry 20% of the global seaborne trade, which represents 19.89% of the total deadweight tonnage and 49.15% of the total EU fleet.[22] Surprisingly, Greek shipping did not follow the global trend and newbuilding orders did not decrease as they did in other countries. Another important factor that makes Greek shipping fundamental to both the Greek economy and the global economy is that the Greek fleet has had the least amount of documented accidents and has the international reputation as being the safest fleet.[23]

Generally, the Greek shipping industry appears to be independent from Greece's domestic sociopolitical and financial situation. Perceptions of the shipowners' status within Greece by different political groups can also be problematic, inciting restrictive and costly government policies.

New governments almost always lead to changes and in Greece they also usually lead to a barrage of accusations from the newly elected against the prior government. Although in some cases the accusations are true, such behavior is bad for business and thus affects all of the country's industries.

NOTES

1 Harlaftis, Gelina. "Greek Commercial and Maritime Networks: The 'Chiot' Phase, 1830s–1860s." In *A History of Greek-Owned Shipping: The Making of an International Tramp Fleet, 1830 to the Present Day*, 39–69. London: Routledge, 2005.
2 "Chios to Izmir." *Distance between Cities Places on Map Distance Calculator*. Last modified December 6, 2019. www.distancefromto.net/.
Illustration 9.1 from www.googlemaps.com.
3 Harlaftis, Gelina. "Greek Commercial and Maritime Networks: The 'Chiot' Phase, 1830s–1860s." In *A History of Greek-Owned Shipping: The Making of an International Tramp Fleet, 1830 to the Present Day*, 39–69. London: Routledge, 2005.
4 Harlaftis, Gelina. "Greek Commercial and Maritime Networks: The 'Chiot' Phase, 1830s–1860s." In *A History of Greek-Owned Shipping: The Making of an International Tramp Fleet, 1830 to the Present Day*, 39–69. London: Routledge, 2005.
5 Muhammad Ali (1769–1849) was the ruler of Egypt from 1805 to 1848, under him Egypt transitioned to its modern independent state. He has been critiqued due to his administrative and economic reforms as he ensured his family's wellbeing and future ruling over the general good; needs which by the mid-1830s we increased due to his military campaigns. Under his ruling most of the Egyptian agriculture was under state control and funds were available to Muhammad Ali. Moreover, he introduced cotton as an agricultural product, which at the time promised high cash returns. He

failed to establish a modern industrial system, mostly because Egypt lacked power sources. The agricultural sector also deteriorated due to mismanagement, high taxation as well as his monopolization of trade.

6 Illustration 9.2 from www.googlemaps.com.

7 Harlaftis, Gelina. "Greek Commercial and Maritime Networks: The 'Chiot' Phase, 1830s–1860s." In *A History of Greek-Owned Shipping: The Making of an International Tramp Fleet, 1830 to the Present Day*, 39–69. London: Routledge, 2005.

8 Crimean War (October 1853—February 1856) took place mostly on the Crimean Peninsula between Russia and the British, French and Ottomans, with the occasional involvement of other countries. The war ended with the Treaty of Paris, according to which the Black Sea was neutralized and the Danube River was opened to the shipping of all nations.

9 Harlaftis, Gelina. "Greek Maritime and Commercial Networks: The 'Ionian' Phase, 1870s–1900s." In *A History of Greek-Owned Shipping: The Making of an International Tramp Fleet, 1830 to the Present Day*, 70–103. London: Routledge, 2005.

10 Harlaftis, Gelina. "Greek Maritime and Commercial Networks: The 'Ionian' Phase, 1870s–1900s." In *A History of Greek-Owned Shipping: The Making of an International Tramp Fleet, 1830 to the Present Day*, 70–103. London: Routledge, 2005.

11 Harlaftis, Gelina. "Greek Maritime 'Expansion', 1914–39." In *A History of Greek-Owned Shipping: The Making of an International Tramp Fleet, 1830 to the Present Day*, 181–206. London: Routledge, 2005.

12 Harlaftis, Gelina. "Greek Maritime 'Expansion', 1914–39." In *A History of Greek-Owned Shipping: The Making of an International Tramp Fleet, 1830 to the Present Day*, 181–206. London: Routledge, 2005.

13 Theotokas, I., and G. Harlaftis. *Leadership in World Shipping: Greek Family Firms in International Business*. Basingstoke: Springer, 2009.

14 "Burial on Skorpios." *The New York Times: Breaking News, World News & Multimedia*. Last modified March 16, 1975. www.nytimes.com/1975/03/16/archives/burial-on-skorpios-aristotle-onassis-dies-of-pneumonia-at-american.html.

15 Theotokas, I., and G. Harlaftis. *Leadership in World Shipping: Greek Family Firms in International Business*. Basingstoke: Springer, 2009.

16 Theotokas, I., and G. Harlaftis. *Leadership in World Shipping: Greek Family Firms in International Business*. Basingstoke: Springer, 2009.

17 Maritimeatgreenwich. "Greek Shipping 1945–2010: A Success Story of Tradition, Innovation, Modernisation." *Maritime at Greenwich*. Last modified October 21, 2013. https://maritimeatgreenwich.wordpress.com/2013/10/21/greek-shipping-1945-2010-a-success-story-of-tradition-innovation-modernisation/.

18 Bergin, T. *How Greek Shipowners Talk Up Their Role, and Why That Costs Athens Millions*. November 25, 2015. Last modified November 9, 2018. www.reuters.com/investigates/special-report/eurozone-greece-shipping/.

19 Bergin, Tom. "The Great Greek Shipping Myth." *Reuters*. Last modified November 25, 2015. www.reuters.com/investigates/special-report/eurozone-greece-shipping/.

20 "Greek Shipowners Agree to Pay 75 Million Euros Annually to State." *U.S.* Last modified February 27, 2019. www.reuters.com/article/greece-shipping-taxation/greek-shipowners-agree-to-pay-75-million-euros-annually-to-state-idUSL5N20M60E.

21 Union of Greek Shipowners. *Greek Shipping and Economy 2016*. Last modified November 9, 2018. www.ugs.gr/en/greek-shipping-and-economy/greek-shipping-and-economy-2016/.

22 Union of Greek Shipowners. *Greek Shipping and Economy 2018*. Last modified November 9, 2018. www.ugs.gr/en/greek-shipping-and-economy/greek-shipping-and-economy-2018/.

23 "Greek Shipping and Economy 2019: The Strategic and Economic Role of Greek Shipping | Hellenic Shipping News Worldwide." *Hellenic Shipping News Worldwide, Online Daily Newspaper on Hellenic and International Shipping*. Last modified August 6, 2019. www.hellenicshippingnews.com/greek-shipping-and-economy-2019-the-strategic-and-economic-role-of-greek-shipping/.

Chapter 10

Road to Privatization

Bad management and misuse of funds have always been crucial issues for Greece. During the Papandreou period, the public sector created a hole in the country's economy. When a government is faced with such problems, there are two options which seem to be the swiftest and most effective. Either the public sector must be reduced considerably, for example, through mass firing, or it must be partially or fully privatized. Prime Minister Karamanlis realized this well before the 2008 economic crisis.

Although it was not the first time a Greek government had to privatize, Karamanlis attempted to strategically privatize. As soon as Karamanlis became the Prime Minister, he privatized a large sector of Greek banking, including Greece's National Bank. Moreover, OTE was partially privatized and Olympic Air, Greece's public airline, was fully privatized by 2009. Overall, from 2004 until 2008, the profits of all privatizations were 6,67 billion Euros, of which approximately 77% came from foreign investments.[1] Once more, investors from all over the world were attracted to Greece because they began to trust the country's economy.

In this context, Prime Minister Karamanlis visited Beijing in January 2006 to meet with his Chinese counterpart, Hu Jintao. Their meeting was considered[2] a diplomatic success as the two men discussed both commercial and cultural matters.[3] One of the subjects examined was an agreement between the two countries, which would directly connect them. More specifically, they proposed to mutually benefit by the use of ports in both countries as transit centers.

The original proposal was verbally made to COSCO's CEO Wei Jiafu, who, a few years later, gave an interview to Alexis Papachelas[4] on the subject. During this interview, Wei Jiafu said that it was simple and Prime Minister Karamanlis stated the importance of COSCO in the shipping world and invited the company to create a direct route from China's port to Greece's ports. Wei Jiafu mentioned in his interview that he would accept the invitation as long as the Greek government was open to include COSCO in Piraeus's privatization.[5]

The first step was made during Prime Minister Karamanlis's visit; however, an official deal was not yet drafted at that time. As a sign of interest and good will, COSCO named their new vessel COSCO HELLAS, registered it under the Greek flag, and held the naming ceremony in Piraeus. During the ceremony, Prime Minister Karamanlis, various ministers, as well as Chinese and Greek officials were present. In his interview, Wei Jiafu mentioned that once the ceremony had ended he approached Prime Minister Karamanlis and asked him to keep up his end of the deal as China had. A few months later, COSCO, in a bidding contest organized by the Greek government, won the rights to the port. The commencement of the project, however, was not easy.

Two years later, in May 2008, the first proposals on how COSCO was envisioning the port and their investment plan were handed in and a long-term deal was drafted. In November of the same year, COSCO Pacific signed a concession agreement with PPA in order to be able to use the container terminal there. The importance of the agreement was obvious since both the Chinese President, Hu Jintao, and Greek Prime Minister, Konstantinos Karamanlis, were present.

Within 24 hours of the signing, all of the port's syndicates organized a strike against the deal. It is important to point out that Alexis Tsipras, who had just become leader of SYRIZA had stated (freely translated) *"the government of New Democracy, along with our parliament's keys is submitting to the Chinese the keys of our Piraeus port. The deal must be cancelled."*[6]

Due to the people's unrest as well as the change of government in Greece, neither joint visit nor statement by officials happened until 2010. In October of that year, Premier Wen Jiabao along with Prime Minister Papandreou expressed their satisfaction with the achievements of the collaboration and their hopes for the future. The two men held a meeting at the presidential house and then visited the port facilities. Premier Wen summarized their meeting in a five-point proposal encouraging bilateral trade and economic relations. One of his points was to deepen the marine transport cooperation. More specifically, and as published by the Chinese embassy in the United States, "China will set up a China–Greece special fund on ship development to provide a package of financial support for Greek shipowners to buy Chinese ships and rejuvenate the bilateral marine transport cooperation. The two sides will expand the throughput of Piraeus port and build the port into a distribution and transit center of Chinese exports of cargo to the EU; strengthen the bilateral coordination and cooperation in the international marine field, establish the China-Greece research center of marine transport energy efficiency and emission reduction and boost the sustainable development of marine transport industry."[7]

During the next five years, this would be proven, to some extent, true. COSCO leased half of the Greek port and transformed it from a state-run enterprise to a private prospering business. Under its management, the port's traffic more than doubled within a year, which lead to more tax income for the Greek government.[8] In 2015, however, Prime Minister Tsipras announced the cancellation of the deal together with all other privatizations. Due to his previous statements, such actions were somewhat expected, though unreasonable given the success of the joint venture. A month later, Prime Minister Tsipras withdrew his previous statement and his Minister of Economics, Yanis Varoufakis, reassured investors that the government was no longer interested in cancelling the deal.[9]

A year later, in April 2016, the final deal between PPA and the COSCO Group was signed, consisting of 51% of the Piraeus Port for €280.5 million. However, the deal was not ratified by the Greek parliament until June of the same year, generating complaints on COSCO's side; it was immediately ready to invest up to €500 million in improving cruise as well as container facilities.[10] COSCO's plan is to increase its stakes by 16%, from 51% to 67% within the next five years, something that would require investments up to €300 million as well as €88 million to the Hellenic Republic Asset Development Fund (HRADF).[11]

Unfortunately, even though COSCO had a positive impact in the terminal's operations, the Greek public sector did not cooperate. Upon their arrival in Greece, COSCO executives revealed their ambitious masterplan, which was to create Piraeus into both a commercial center and a tourist attraction. To accomplish this, COSCO planned to further develop and modernize the cruise ship terminal. Moreover, they planned on building four hotels as well as a shopping center.[12] Finally, COSCO committed to further develop existing commercial terminals and also to create a new container terminal. The estimated total investment by COSCO is at €800 million,[13] of which €300 million must be invested by the end of 2022.[14]

In early 2019, however, the *Central Committee of Archeology and Museums* (CCAM) declared Piraeus an area of archeological interest and therefore forbade all developments current and future. CCAM is a subdivision of the Ministry of Culture and Sports and was established in 1834. The committee's main goal is to prevent exploitation of area of historical importance. Although, undeniably, CCAM is of great importance, members of the committee should apply some critical eye when examining areas. Due to Greece's long history, it is almost impossible to dig anywhere in Greece and especially in Attika without finding any trace of the country's ancient history. Therefore, and because it is a part of the government, the CCAM has been used on various occasions as a pretense to stop projects of which governments were not in favor. In the case of Piraeus, CCAM froze the investment[15] claiming that the development would be made in a distance shorter than the predicted distance. Such development, of course, upset COSCO management who shortly after this was announced signed a deal with the port of Trieste in Italy.[16]

Fortunately, then Minister of Culture, Mirsini Zormpa, did not go through with CCAM's report and the investment will continue as planned. In late August 2019, COSCO submitted to the newly elected government the official proposal for its masterplan. The Greek government was asked to approve a €612 million, including funding for a new mall, which the previous government had rejected in favor of small local businesses. This time COSCO's masterplan was approved.

The proposal of such an investment is also seen as a vote of confidence in the newly elected government.

NOTES

1 Λουκέρη, Σοφία. *Κώστας Καραμανλής, Το Τελευταίο Εμπόδιο.* Αθήνα: Ιππόκαμπος Εκδόσεις, 2017.
2 Λουκέρη, Σοφία. *Κώστας Καραμανλής, Το Τελευταίο Εμπόδιο.* Αθήνα: Ιππόκαμπος Εκδόσεις, 2017.
3 "China-Greece Relations in 'Best' Period since Diplomatic Ties Forged: President Hu." *The State Council the People's Republic of China.* n.d. www.gov.cn/misc/2006-01/20/content_166056.htm.
4 Alexis Papachelas is a Greek investigative journalist and current Executive Editor of Kathimerini newspaper.
5 Λουκέρη, Σοφία. *Κώστας Καραμανλής, Το Τελευταίο Εμπόδιο.* Αθήνα: Ιππόκαμπος Εκδόσεις, 2017.
6 Λουκέρη, Σοφία. *Κώστας Καραμανλής, Το Τελευταίο Εμπόδιο.* Αθήνα: Ιππόκαμπος Εκδόσεις, 2017.

7 "Premier Wen Jiabao Meets with Greek Prime Minister George Papandreou." *Embassy of the People's Republic of China in the United States of America*. 2010. www. china-embassy.org/eng/zgyw/t759474.htm.

8 Alderman, Liz. "Chinese Company Sets New Rhythm in Port of Piraeus." *The New York Times: Breaking News, World News & Multimedia*. Last modified October 10, 2012. www.nytimes.com/2012/10/11/business/global/chinese-company-sets-new-rhythm-in-port-of-piraeus.html.

9 Meunier, Sophie. "A Tale of Two Ports: The Epic Story of Chinese Direct Investment in the Greek Port of Piraeus." *CritCom | A Forum for Research and Commentary on Europe*. Last modified December 14, 2015. https://critcom.councilforeuropeanstudies.org/a-tale-of-two-ports-the-epic-story-of-chinese-direct-investment-in-the-greek-port-of-piraeus/.

10 Georgiopoulos, George. "China's Cosco Acquires 51 Pct Stake in Greece's Piraeus Port." *Reuters*. Last modified August 10, 2016. www.reuters.com/article/greece-privatisation-port/chinas-cosco-acquires-51-pct-stake-in-greeces-piraeus-port-idUSL8N1AR252.

11 Georgiopoulos, George. "China's Cosco Acquires 51 Pct Stake in Greece's Piraeus Port." *U.S.* Last modified August 10, 2016. www.reuters.com/article/greece-privatisation-port/chinas-cosco-acquires-51-pct-stake-in-greeces-piraeus-port-idUSL8N1AR252.

12 Bellos, Ilias. "Cosco's Piraeus Plan Approved, in Part." *Ekathimerini.com*. Last modified October 13, 2019. www.ekathimerini.com/245471/article/ekathimerini/business/coscos-piraeus-plan-approved-in-part.

13 www.ekathimerini.com/243778/article/ekathimerini/business/piraeus-port-owner-cosco-to-submit-investment-plan.

14 "China, Greece Agree to Push Ahead with COSCO's Piraeus Port Investment." *U.S.* Last modified November 11, 2019. www.reuters.com/article/us-greece-china/china-greece-agree-to-push-ahead-with-coscos-piraeus-port-investment-idUSKBN1XL1KC.

15 Konstandaras, Nikos. "Who Is Playing Politics with the Port of Piraeus?" *The New York Times: Breaking News, World News & Multimedia*. Last modified May 23, 2019. www.nytimes.com/2019/05/23/opinion/piraeus-greece-china.html.

16 Ullyett, Richard. "COSCO Signs Agreement with Another Mediterranean Port." *PortSEurope*. Last modified February 12, 2019. www.portseurope.com/cosco-signs-agreement-with-another-mediterranean-port/.

Chapter 11

Insider's View

An accurate and in-depth understanding of the Greek–COSCO deal about Piraeus, and its consequences, depends on understanding how the deal was perceived by important public groups and individuals. Thus, this chapter focuses on interviews I personally made from late 2018 and 2019.[1] I consider my interview of George Gogos, General Secretary of the PPA Dockers Union, as one of the most valuable. Mr. Gogos has worked as a docker since 2005, entered the administration of the union in 2009, and offers some of the most perceptive comments representative of labor.

As he pointed out during our interview, when a docker is elected as a representative of the union he is exempted from his duties as a worker. All representatives of the union are paid by the *Piraeus Port Authority* (PPA) and once their tenure is complete they return to their previous positions. As Mr. Gogos mentioned, their main activities are neither covered by the news nor known to many people. As is the case at all ports, Piraeus does not stop operations on Sundays or holidays. One of the union's main tasks is to allocate and, in some cases, even persuade individuals to come to work on such days. Moreover, they are responsible for defending the rights and interests of the dockers.

The PPA Dockers Union is one of four operating within the port. The Dockworkers Union of Piraeus was originally founded in 1925. Since then their activities stopped various occasions during the turbulent history of the Greek nation. In 1968, the Union was reformed and was reestablished in today's form. Since then the Union has been considered one of the strongest in Greece as it is responsible for the smooth operation of the port.

When asked about the deal, Mr. Gogos answered that it was affecting various aspects of the dockers' lives, saying that the union's involvement and position was made clear from the very beginning when Prime Minister Karamanlis and the Chinese President Hu Jintao were discussing the bilateral agreement for a direct trading line. According to the original concept, the whole port would have been bought by COSCO, something that the union viewed as threatening, because everyone could potentially be fired. No such agreement was signed as it generated objections from the EU as well as the local unions.

When the negotiations for the *Piraeus Container Terminal—Σταθμός Εμπορευματοκιβωτίων Πειραιά* (PCT) were completed and COSCO took it over, there was no established union representing the PCT workers, unlike that representing the PPA workers which was established since 1925. As expected, COSCO was initially against any such establishment but through time not one but three unions were established. Although the nature of employers and employees is in opposing each other, as Mr. Gogos points out, the union is nothing more than a collective representation of workers.

Moreover, since COSCO became a new employer and was unaware of how things functioned in Greece, the unions would have provided them with valuable insight. Neither the dockers' union nor the unions established within the PCT aim for endless strikes and try to solve problems through an open dialogue between them and the administration. Gogos's argument is supported by the fact that the workers' salaries are directly dependent on the daily hours worked. If they do not work they do not get paid. This contradicts the purpose of the union and differentiates them from all other Greek unions whose salaries are not dependent upon the actual hours worked.

Since COSCO took over, the unions have collaborated and organized a few daily strikes. Considering the cultural differences the two sides have, their contrasting ways of approach, and the sheer quantity of changes that COSCO originally wanted to implement, there have been few strikes. According to Mr. Gogos, this smooth transition was accomplished because the deal for this part of the port had a clause which clearly stated that whatever changes the new administration wants to make must be mutually agreed.

Moreover, due to the good organization of the workers and their unity, negotiations were overall considered a success by both sides. A major issue was the fact that the new Chinese administration was not familiar with the prevailing laws and customs following Piraeus. However, both sides are learning to work with each other.

A fact the union soon became aware of was that they were no longer negotiating with the government. Thus, their techniques and overall approach changed shortly after COSCO took over. Mr. Gogos also pointed out that some issues were solved faster due to the decreased bureaucracy and corruption.

All is not perfect; on other issues, bureaucracy has increased. There are certain decisions that must go through not only the local COSCO administration but also through the central administration in China. At this point during the interview, a comparison was made between the understanding of the two sides.

Locally, Captain Fu Cheng Qui, who has been responsible for the smooth operations in Greece and the expansion of the piers, has developed an understanding and awareness of how things happen. Moreover, his personal assistant, who has studied in Thessaloniki and is fluent in Greek, often helps breach any communication gap between the two sides.[2] Through constant work from both sides, each is aware of the limits, needs, and wants of the other side.

On the other hand, the administration sitting in China neither has personal contact with nor is able to comprehend the Piraeus reality. This gap between the two COSCO organs frequently creates delay because there is a constant back and forth explaining or justifying the same issue.

A fortunate similarity between the new, private, and old, public, administration is the efficiency in paying salaries. Although this is expected of a private company, especially one of such size, efficient payment from Greece's public sector has not always been a given. Because COSCO is an arm of the Chinese government with the mission of implementing state capitalism, it obviously wants to maximize its profit. To do so, COSCO has tried to intensify the work schedule at the port. Due to the nature and transparency of the dockers' work, COSCO's plans were not initially rejected by the dockers. As Mr. Gogos explained during the interview, Greek dockers are organized in teams and each team is responsible for its own part. Their day consists of eight hours but they are paid on a quantity basis, not an hourly basis. Therefore, the more they load or unload the more they earn. But in some cases, COSCO's requests have been unrealistic, creating the discomfort and negative reaction of the workers. COSCO was expecting the dockers to have an even more intense work schedule, ignoring the fact that their job is manual labor and there are and should be limits. Understandably, this led to a major conflict between the two sides.

As if this conflict was not enough, COSCO also changed their workable days. It is customary in Greece to work Monday to Friday and be paid overtime for any weekend and holiday worked. However, COSCO now expected workers to labor five days a week but their days off could be any day of the week, including a weekday. This request may be perceived as logical since vessels arrive any and every day of the year. However, due to cultural and religious reasons, Sundays are traditionally considered an important family day in Greece. Since, however, COSCO is Chinese and did not share this tradition they did not consider it in the beginning.

Prior to COSCO's involvement, Piraeus port was operating almost every day and there were always dockers working and being compensated with overtime pay for sacrificing those weekend days. With COSCO's modification, however, this motivation was gone since weekends are now considered and paid like any other day of the week. To enforce any change, both sides must agree, and this is no exception. Once COSCO's final proposal was presented the union voted and decided to move forward with this new arrangement.

This proposal also contained a win for the union. Originally, COSCO wanted to outsource most of the services provided within the port, and outsourcing, of course, meant that many of the employees would be fired. Additionally, COSCO would not be responsible for the actual employee's needs, insurance, salary, and so on, but would only have to pay the company contracted. This, as discussed in the interview, is acceptable for services such as cleaning and security, but not for the core business. In mid-2019, both sides finally came to an agreement that satisfied each.

The aforementioned cases are only two examples of the constant give and take between the parties. Mr. Gogos pointed out that during the past three years the relationship between the two sides has significantly improved. Gogos indicated that as a union representative, and also on a personal level, he is rather optimistic about future cooperation.

His optimism, however, somewhat faded once asked about COSCO's mega plan. He pointed out that it is not right to mix port related and non-related activities. He is worried that COSCO will exploit the port as well as the whole area and therefore the balance between port and non-port related activities will be lost. This mega plan, in his eyes, threatens the local small businesses as well as the efficiency of the port. He did mention that there is a need for a parking space and this might be more useful instead of building two large hotels in the area. Moreover, he remains hesitant on whether the profits will be invested back to the port and therefore further increase profits. Since the new management took over, there is an undeniable increase in work as well as in profit. However, as he added, it remains to be seen if this increase will benefit the workers, or as it is more likely in his opinion, be contrary to their interests.

Closing his interview, Mr. Gogos expressed that the workers do feel confident that whatever they have agreed upon will materialize. Moreover, the two sides are working on making the port a safer place primarily for the people but also for the cargo. One of his final comments was that the OBOR initiative is in desperate need of a success story and Piraeus might be it.

NOTES

1 All Interviews were held by the author, Tatiana Gontika, either in person, over the phone, or by email during said period.
2 Thessaloniki, the second biggest city after Athens and also a port city, is located in the North of the country and is considered the second most important city in Greece.

Chapter 12

The Expansion

Is the Piraeus port deal a success story? The answer to that question depends on the evaluation of some major aspects.

The most import evaluation must be of the impact that the deal has on the people closely connected to the port and its operations. As Mr. Gogos explained during his interview, the dockers' union and COSCO have signed an agreement according to which two-thirds of the dockers will have a permanent position. The other one-third will be contracted, workload permitting. This agreement was satisfactory for two main reasons: (1) Piraeus traffic has increased and soon there will be need for more dockers; and (2) one of the port's main activities, the cruises, are seasonal, therefore it is logical for COSCO to have to contract. Having a relatively long summer, Greece attracts cruise ships approximately eight months a year, though the busiest months are, without doubt, May–September. Since this agreement was negotiated during May–June 2019, it remains to be seen how it will be implemented in the next season.

Another issue that Mr. Gogos pointed out is that although COSCO had unrealistic expectations on workload they were not willing to pay overtime. In some cases, operations would stop at the end of the working day and therefore vessels would have to wait. This contradicts COSCO's basis for terminating traditional weekends off in favor of their any-five-day work week under the auspices of the aforementioned logic of vessels arriving on any day. This preference of paying salaries and not overtime seems in line with the dockers' request of permanently hiring the remaining one-third. In my opinion, the only threat this one-third faces are external contractors with more competitive requests. However, most dockers working in the port have been there for over five years and are very experienced, thus making them almost irreplaceable for the smooth operation of the port. There has not been any mass firing and people are conservatively optimistic.

One of the issues and an undeniable fact is that COSCO is not a Greek company and does not represent Greek interests. It is the view of many, that the Greek government sold out one of the country's most profitable SOEs. However, this is not entirely true. The Greek state needed cash and a reduction of expenses. Although the port was always covering its expenses, no investment had been made toward its improvement for at least ten years. On the other hand, even though COSCO is not Greek and represents different interests they do benefit from the operation of the port as much, if not more, than the Greek people. As Mr. George Alexandratos, Deputy Chairman of the Greek Chamber of Shipping, said during his interview:

> Well speaking personally, I always try to defend and keep as much as possible under Greek control the properties and sectors of business environment. But we cannot ignore (whether we like it or not) that we are under a competitive "globalized" economy and China is one of the most powerful partners and definitely one of the fastest developing countries.

China, as established elsewhere in this paper, is trying to become a superpower and to do so it needs an entrance to the Balkans and an intermodal corridor from the eastern Mediterranean to northern and western Europe. COSCO, actually an arm of the Chinese state, is directly representing those interests. Therefore, and as long as no drastic changes are made from the Greek side, Piraeus will not become a secondary project to either the Chinese or Greece.

Other interviewees, such as Christos Avdimiotis, Surveyor in Edvemon & Partners, are not convinced that the deal is in Greece's best interest. During his interview, Mr. Avdimiotis said:

> The long-term contractual agreement between COSCO and the Greek state although at a first glance has yielded considerable earnings to both parties, I would personally consider the particular deal rather questionable as it is quite difficult to compare what would be the profits of the previously profitable management scheme vs the new.

Of course, there is neither a way to accurately predict the future nor is there one to see what would have happened if different decisions were made. It is for this reason that the only way to evaluate the deal is the profit the port generates as well as the working conditions. Since both appear to be to a certain extent positive it is safe to conclude that COSCO, thus China, might get its OBOR success story in Greece.

In addition to the existing jobs, which have not been severely affected, COSCO plans to soon create new jobs. Only a few months after the new Prime Minister Kyriakos Mitsotakis's government took over, COSCO's plan, worth $670 million, was approved. The approved proposal allows COSCO to improve the port's infrastructure, build a new cruise port, and also four hotels among other developments. Although Mr. Gogos's concerns remain about whether the area may support this rapid growth, it is a much-needed investment. Through it, new jobs will open. In addition, new businesses mean new tax income for the indebted government; also, through this investment, the Piraeus area will be updated and probably upgraded.

Another important aspect that must be considered regarding the investment as a whole is its environmental impact. PPA has had a *Port Environmental Review System* (PERS) certification since 2004. The PERS is the only port sector-specific environmental management standard issued by the EcoPorts and its implementation is independently reviewed by Lloyd's Register. PERS is built based on recommendations made by the *European Sea Ports Organization* (ESPO), which provide ports with goals. The certificate is valid for two years and 32 ports have obtained it.[1]

As a member of the initiative and holder of the certificate Piraeus port is actively involved with the *Sustainable Ports in the Adriatic–Ionian Region* (SUPAIR) project.[2] The project initiated in January 2018 and, assuming all goes well, will be completed in December 2019. Its main goal is to develop and implement action plans for the reduction of carbon emissions in European ports, focusing on the Adriatic–Ionian region. The involvement of the port's administration into such initiatives shows some environmental awareness. Along with the administration, the various unions of the port are gathering information in order to research not only the environmental impact their operations have but also the impact on their health as well as of those who live in the surrounding area.

The expansion of the port facilities and operations affects not only the area but also nation at large. Assuming that it does become the success story, it seems on its way to be, then it will become a major gateway from the East to Europe. In order to be able to support a highly trafficked gateway, Greece will have to make a few infrastructural upgrades.

A major project that is already complete is that of Egnatia motorway (*Εγνατία Οδός*). This route is one of the most frequently used to/from Rome. Moreover, it leads to a well-known trading center of both ancient and modern times, Istanbul. Today, the motorway links Greece with bordering Albania, FYROM, Bulgaria, and Turkey. The last part of the project was completed in 2014 and since then traveling time within Greece has significantly dropped. Moreover, Egnatia motorway is part of a larger international road network, linking the country with Balkan and European countries. Thus, Piraeus is directly connected to the most important highways in the region.[3]

Unlike the highways connecting Greece to the rest of Europe, the country's rail system has been suffering. The 2008 financial crisis severely affected and ultimately led to the suspension of all international routes in 2011.[4] However, in 2014, two of the international lines were reestablished. The first from Thessaloniki to Skopje and the second from Thessaloniki to Sofia. In August 2015 though, because of the refugee crisis, the line from Thessaloniki to Skopje was suspended. On a domestic level, the rail system, though outdated, is rather reliable. There are trains connecting some of the country's major cities. The most popular among tourists, and for cargo shippers, is the overnight train from Athens to Thessaloniki. The line running within the city of Athens, connecting Kifissia to Piraeus works fairly well and is used by both locals and tourists.[5] Therefore, the domestic rail system, even though requiring renovation and investment, is reliable and functional.

In an attempt to further link and optimize transportation of both goods and people, the EU, along with the Greek Ministry of Infrastructure, Transport and Networks, is currently designing the *Egnatia Railway* project. The railway will run in parallel with the Egnatia Motorway and will similarly connect Northern Greece. Upon completion of this project, the Greek railway will be linked to the Bulgarian as well as the Albanian railways. Additionally, northern Greek ports, such as the Alexandroupolis port, will have direct access to rail, similar to the Piraeus port.

A strong Greek transportation network will be established once the railway project is complete, along with the existing highway network and the modernization and further development of Piraeus port. Because Piraeus port will most probably be the heart of transportation operations, and the Piraeus port investment is part of the OBOR initiative, the Chinese ambition for a strong presence in Europe will be accomplished. As Mr. Alexandratos mentioned in his interview:

I presume that if Greece has the possibility to maximize the potential of this project then it will revive its stagnated national economy. I think we are all slowly starting to realize that China wants Greece to become the gate for all the Chinese products in Europe due to our geographical position.

Such an accomplishment will affect other European ports and probably the EU as a whole. As China will have increased not only its geopolitical power but also its economic influence over Asia now it will do the same in Europe. Various cities in the Netherlands, Germany, Denmark, and other northern European countries will be greatly affected as they will no longer be the entrance of the corridor into central Europe but instead, the ending. Those cities stand to lose commercial importance.

Another reason why these mentioned countries might see this deal as a threat is because of the increased number of vessels calling at the Piraeus port, which has resulted in other ports experiencing a decrease in the number of vessels calling. One of the ports to be very affected will be Rotterdam, which is one of Europe's most important and busiest ports. For vessels coming from the East, it will no longer make sense to sail all the way to the Netherlands in order to distribute their products to central Europe once Greece provides a more convenient alternative. Rotterdam is only an example; there are many Western European cities that will be negatively affected by such changes.

Simultaneously, countries neighboring Greece will benefit from Greece's good fortune directly and indirectly. First and foremost, neighboring countries will now become the ancillary to the East's entrance into central Europe and northern Europe, and an essential part of the route. As the Greek economy grows, more opportunities will be created for both Greeks and foreigners willing to move to Greece. Historically, before the crisis, people from almost all of Greece's neighboring countries emigrated to Greece for better job opportunities and they might be able to do the same again soon.[6]

On a large scale of analysis, it is clear from the Piraeus case that the OBOR initiative affects the socioeconomic and political situation of a country and also the environment around it. According to Alexander Pfaff's interview, published by Duke University, there are many environmental implications.[7] There are the direct environmental consequences of building roads or spilling oil on the ground. But there are other long-term consequences generated from the OBOR. The initiative is so elaborate that it will probably lead to the reorganization of cities and thus, economies. In other words, key cities of the OBOR initiative will become hubs for new work opportunities and will attract people to move there. Consequently, they will grow and therefore their pollution, waste, and other environmentally crucial aspects will also increase. Because of high levels of awareness in the recent past, governments and the responsible entities within the private sector are likely to be proactive and will minimize or even prevent such negative consequences.

Another alarming aspect, as published by the *Environmental and Energy Study Institute* (EESI), is that many of the major corridors pass through *Ecologically Sensitive Areas* (ESA). ESA, as defined by the *General Multilingual Environmental Thesaurus,* is any area where it is likely that a change in some parts of the system will produce a recognizable response and irreversible change.[8]

In the OBOR initiative, such areas are found throughout Eurasia. The newly built roads and railways could potentially threaten plants and animals of the surrounding ecosystem. According to the same article, over 265 threatened species will probably be affected. Moreover, deforestation will, inevitably, happen having both immediate and long-term effects.

In May 2017, the World Wildlife Foundation (WWF) published a report titled *The Belt and Road Initiative—WWF Recommendations and Spatial Analysis.* As the title suggests the report focuses on the OBOR initiative and its environmental consequences. Through their report, WWF does not stand against the overall initiative, but states that "if it is not planned carefully, it can have unintended negative environmental consequences, which in turn can jeopardize the success of the project."[9] During its research, WWF focused on six categories: threatened species, ESAs, protected areas, water-related ecosystem services, wilderness characteristics, and finally the overall impact. The map illustrates areas that will be impacted more severly than others. Areas in surrounding and including Thailand, parts of China and Mongolia as well as areas in the Middle East will be severly impacted. (see Figure 12.1).[10] The areas included in the corridor running through Russia and Northen Europe will experience lower impact. However, they should not be considered danger-free zones because they too form part of the surrounding ecosystems.

The WWF study has nine recommendations. The first three concern the system level design. In the first one, their suggestion is to plan and implement within the context of ecological civilization and sustainable development goal. The next focuses on the enhanced monitoring and annual evaluation of each individual project. The third, and final one in

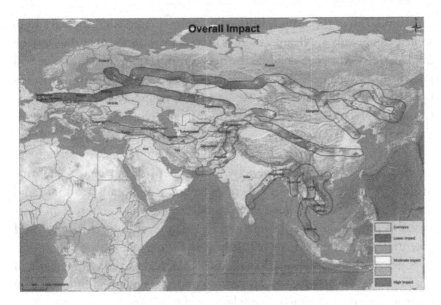

FIGURE 12.1
OBOR Environmental Impact.

this category, focuses on investments toward ecological infrastructure and renewable energy infrastructure.

The second category of recommendations is on sector level planning, which consists of four sets. First, tools to assist decision-making, such as *Strategic Environmental Assessments*, should be used and natural capital approaches mush be applied. Additionally, ESAs must be identified and mapped to evaluate opportunities for ecological infrastructure. A direct result of this is the next recommendation, according to which sustainable supply chain management must be promoted. Finally, local authorities must be involved and responsible to ensure that such measures are being enforced.

The third and fourth categories each consist of one recommendation. The project-level planning and implementation recommendation encourage funding from international institutions, such as the World Bank and the International Finance Corporation. Attention is also drawn on the implementation of international law and standards.[11] The final category relates to governance and transparency issues, focusing on transparency and inclusion of the local governments. Finally, science, technology, and an environmental protection platform must be established and respected by all, irrespective of their socioeconomic background.

Although all of the aforementioned recommendations are logical and to some extent easily applicable, there is no certainty on whether they will be implemented. Moreover, China, the mastermind behind the initiative will most probably be uneasy to surrendering any type of control to any institution with which they are not actively and heavily involved. Unfortunately, China has a recorded lack of clear commitment and enforcement in health and environmental matters.[12]

However, due to China's domestic environmental decay, mostly due to rapid economic growth, there is hope that they will not make the same mistakes outside their country. Furthermore, it is because of this rapid growth that they are in need of natural resources and therefore, will most probably protect the ones in which they have interest. Chinese needs could potentially turn into threats for these ESAs if overexploitation develops. In conclusion, the only way to make sure that negative consequences will not happen is by governments following and implementing international environmental and infrastructure laws, and guidelines.

NOTES

1 "Network." *Welcome: EcoPorts | ESPO*. Last modified December 3, 2019. www.ecoports.com/network.

2 "Sustainable Ports in the Adriatic-Ionian Region." *European Union*. 2018. https://supair.adrioninterreg.eu/.

3 "Trains in Greece." *RailPass.com | Eurail and Europe Rail Pass Experts*. Accessed December 3, 2019. http://www.railpass.com/trains/greece.

4 "Trains in Greece." *RailPass.com | Eurail and Europe Rail Pass Experts*. Last modified December 3, 2019. www.railpass.com/trains/greece.

5 Kifissia: Suburb in the North of Athens.

6 Albania, North Macedonia, and Bulgaria.

7 Duke University. "China's One Belt, One Road Plan Carries Environmental Risks." *Futurity*. Last modified May 10, 2019. www.futurity.org/one-belt-one-road-china-environmental-impact-2058742/.

8 European Environment Information and Observation Network: Eionet Portal. "Ecologically Sensitive Area." *General Multilingual Environmental Thesaurus*. n.d. Last modified December 3, 2019. www.eionet.europa.eu/gemet/en/concept/2461.

9 "The Belt and Road Initiative WWF Recommendations and Spatial Analysis." *WWF*. Last modified May 2017. http://awsassets.panda.org/downloads/the_belt_and_road_initiative___wwf_recommendations_and_spatial_analysis___may_2017.pdf.

10 Illustration 12.1 from: WWF UK (2017), The Belt and Road Initiative WWF Recommendations and Spatial Analysis.

11 Illustration 12.1 from: WWF UK (2017), The Belt and Road Initiative WWF Recommendations and Spatial Analysis.
12 Globalization Monitor. "What Does 'China's One Belt, One Road' Might Means for
the Environment?" *Intercoll*. Last modified February 11, 2019. https://intercoll.net/
What-does-China-s-One-Belt-One-Road-might-means-for-the-environment.

Conclusion

If it is true that history does, indeed, repeat itself then both Greece and China shall become major players in international trade and the world's economy. China has established itself throughout its modern history. Greece, however, faces various difficulties, especially political and economic. Other than their rich history, the two countries share the common interest of shipping. Greece historically has been a maritime country, having some of the world's most important shipowners. Chinese shipping, on the other hand, has not had such a steady path through the years. However, in the past few decades, China has become one of the major hubs for new building and trading. Therefore, it is of no surprise that the two countries are collaborating in building a financial and commercial future together.

COSCO, one variable of the equation, represents Chinese interests. The company was originally part of the government. Upon its denationalization, it remained very much influenced by it and today is considered as a direct associate of the Chinese government. The second variable, representing the Greek interests, is PPA. Piraeus port has a strategic location and has always been a busy and efficient port. This collaboration is part of the bigger international OBOR initiative. The Chinese expansion policies are particularly evident in Greece, Pakistan, and Djibouti. But it is not limited to them, as almost a third of the world's countries will be affected.

The OBOR initiative is a modern version of the Silk Road network aiming to optimize trading and strengthening China's position in the global market. Three main alternative routes, the northern and southern land and the maritime, are being considered, each of them with numerous variations. Piraeus is considered a key location for both the southern land as well as the maritime route as it will be China's entrance into the Balkans and the rest of Europe.

The Chinese government realized Piraeus's importance and the first approach between the two governments happened in early 2006. Since then Greece's economic and sociopolitical situation changed various times. These changes affected not only the people on a local level but, on some occasions, the smooth cooperation between the two countries. Fortunately, during the second half of 2019 Sino–Greek relations have further tightened and high-ranked government members of both countries are very optimistic for what the future holds. President Xi Jinping and the Prime Minister Kyriakos Mitsotakis held a joint visit to Piraeus port during President Xi's official visit in November 2019.

COSCO's investment and involvement in Piraeus port, so far, has been successful. Even individuals who initially were against this deal, such as members of the dockers' union, are now more optimistic about it. Similarly, the Chinese government is seeing one of the best, so far, results of their OBOR initiative. Thus, there is no reason to believe that this cooperation will not continue to be mutually beneficial. Although certain concerns such as the environment and the local markets have risen, the further investments that are meant to be completed within the next years should not be boycotted or postponed for Greece's benefit.

On the other hand, some control must exist, because the EU and the whole world is anxiously waiting to see how the OBOR initiative will evolve. Although there is no way to accurately predict the future, if the OBOR initiative is fulfilled the international markets will change significantly. China will probably become the most important player as they will be controlling a major fraction of international trade.

Glossary

Automatic Identification System	AIS
China National Offshore Oil Corp	CNOO
China Ocean Shipping Company	COSCO
China State Construction Engineering Corp	CSCEC
China–Pakistan Economic Corridor	CPEC
Chinese Ministry of Communication	MOC
Coalition of Radical Left	SYRIZA
Deadweight Tonnage	DWT
Ecologically Sensitive Areas	ESA
Electronic Chart Display and Information System	ECDIS
Environmental and Energy Study Institute	EESI
Eurasian Economic Union	EAEU
European Sea Ports Organization	ESPO
European Union	EU
Former Yugoslav Republic of Macedonia	FYROM
Free and Open Indo-Pacific Strategy	FOIP
Free Trade Agreements	FTA
Free Trade Zone	FTZ
Greek Civil War	GCW
Greek Communist Party	KKE
Greek Democratic Army	DSE
Greek Liberation Army	ELAS
Hellenic Telecommunications Organization	OTE
International Maritime Bureau	IMB
International Monetary Fund	IMF
Mega-Regional Trade Agreements	MRTA
Memoranda of Understanding	MOU
National Liberation Front	EAM
National People's Congress	NPC
National Republican Greek League	EDES
New Democracy	ND
One Belt One Road	OBOR
Panhellenic Socialist Movement	PASOK
Piraeus Container Terminal	PCT

Piraeus Port Authority	PPA
Port Environmental Review System	PERS
Special Economic Zones	SEZ
State-Owned Enterprise	SOE
Sustainable Ports in the Adriatic - Ionian Region	SUPAIR
Trans-Anatolian Pipeline	TANAP
Trans-Pacific Partnership	TPP
Union of Greek Shipowners	UGS
Vessel Traffic Service	VTS
World Economic Forum	WEF
World Wildlife Foundation	WWF

Bibliography

"3 Types of Free Trade Agreements and How They Work." *The Balance*. Last modified March 10, 2011. www.thebalance.com/free-trade-agreement-types-and-examples-3305897.

"Γ. Στουρνάρας: Ο ρόλος της ελληνικής ναυτιλίας σήμερα." *Ναυτικά Χρονικά*. Last modified October 22, 2019. www.naftikachronika.gr/2019/10/22/g-stournaras-o-rolos-tis-ellinikis-naftilias-simera/.

"ΔΗΜΟΨΗΦΙΣΜΑ της 5ης Ιουλίου 2015." *Υπουργείο Εσωτερικών*. n.d. www.ypes.gr/UserFiles/f0ff9297-f516-40ff-a70e-eca84e2ec9b9/psfd-referendumB.jpg.

"Ιστορικά Στοιχεία, Ένωση Μονίμων & Δοκίμων Λιμενεργατών Ο.Λ.Π." *Ένωση Μονίμων & Δοκίμων Λιμενεργατών Ο.Λ.Π*. Last modified December 3, 2019. www.dockers.gr/history.

"ΤΑ ΣΥΝΔΙΚΑΤΑ ΞΕΠΟΥΛΗΣΑΝΕ ΤΟ ΛΙΜΑΝΙ ΣΤΗ ΦΑΣΙΣΤΙΚΗ ΚΙΝΑ ΜΕ ΤΗ ΒΟΥΛΑ ΤΟΥ ΚΑΘΕΣΤΩΤΟΣ." *ΟΡΓΑΝΩΣΗ ΓΙΑ ΤΗΝ ΑΝΑΣΥΓΚΡΟΤΗΣΗ ΤΟΥ ΚΚΕ*. Last modified December 3, 2019. www.oakke.gr/na451/chinaolp_451.htm.

Aizhu, Chen. "Exclusive: China in $5 Billion Drive to Develop Disputed East China Sea Gas." *Reuters*. Last modified July 17, 2013. www.reuters.com/article/us-cnooc-eastchinasea-idUSBRE96G0BA20130717.

Alderman, Liz. "Chinese Company Sets New Rhythm in Port of Piraeus." *The New York Times: Breaking News, World News & Multimedia*. Last modified October 10, 2012. www.nytimes.com/2012/10/11/business/global/chinese-company-sets-new-rhythm-in-port-of-piraeus.html.

Arnett, George, Ami Sedghi, Achilleas Galatsidas, and Sean Clarke. "Greek Referendum: Full Results." *The Guardian*. Last modified June 14, 2016. www.theguardian.com/world/ng-interactive/2015/jul/05/live-results-greek-referendum.

Bank, World. *Belt and Road Economics: Opportunities and Risks of Transport Corridors*. Washington: World Bank Publications, 2019.

Barrett, Matt. *History of Greece: Post-War*. n.d. www.ahistoryofgreece.com/post-war.htm.

Baumgartner, Pete. "China's Massive 'One Road' Project Largely Bypasses Russia, But Moscow Still on Board." *RadioFreeEurope/RadioLiberty*. Last modified June 26, 2017. www.rferl.org/a/russia-china-one-belt-one-road-project-putin-xi/28579849.html.

Bellos, Ilias. "Piraeus Port Owner Cosco to Submit Investment Plan, Ilias Bellos | Kathimerini." *Ekathimerini.com*. Last modified August 22, 2019. www.ekathimerini.com/243778/article/ekathimerini/business/piraeus-port-owner-cosco-to-submit-investment-plan.

"Belt and Road Initiative." *Belt and Road Initiative*. Last modified April 29, 2018. www.beltroad-initiative.com/belt-and-road/.

"The Belt and Road Initiative WWF Recommendations and Spatial Analysis." *WWF*. Last modified May. http://awsassets.panda.org/downloads/the_belt_and_road_initiative___wwf_recommendations_and_spatial_analysis___may_2017.pdf.

Bergin, Tom. "How Greek Shipowners Talk Up Their Role, and Why That Costs Athens Millions." *Reuters*. Last modified November 25, 2015. www.reuters.com/investigates/special-report/eurozone-greece-shipping/.

Bnamericas. "Cosco Sees 2020 Construction Start for US$3bn Chancay Port." *BNamericas. com*. Last modified June 26, 2019. www.bnamericas.com/en/news/cosco-sees-2020-construction-start-for-us3bn-chancay-port.

Bosu, Rabi Sankar. "BRI Will Bring China and ASEAN Closer." *China.org.cn: China News, Business, Travel & Language Courses*. Last modified May 22, 2017. www.china.org.cn/opinion/2017-05/22/content_40865507.htm.

Breue, Julia. "Two Belts, One Road? The Role of Africa in China's Belt & Road Initiative." *Stiftung Asienhaus in Köln: Asienhaus.de*. Last modified July 2017. www.asienhaus.de/uploads/tx_news/Blickwechsel_OBOR-Afrika_Maerz2018_03.pdf.

"A Brief History of China's Economic Growth." *World Economic Forum*. Last modified December 4, 2019. www.weforum.org/agenda/2015/07/brief-history-of-china-economic-growth/.

Briney, Amanda. "A Quick Rundown on the History and Geography of Modern China." *ThoughtCo*. Last modified November 20, 2019. www.thoughtco.com/geography-and-modern-history-of-china-1434414.

"Burial on Skorpios." *The New York Times: Breaking News, World News & Multimedia*. Last modified March 16, 1975. www.nytimes.com/1975/03/16/archives/burial-on-skorpios-aristotle-onassis-dies-of-pneumonia-at-american.html.

"Bush Calls for Universal Broadband by 2007." *Msnbc.com*. Last modified March 26, 2004. www.nbcnews.com/id/4609864/ns/technology_and_science-tech_and_gadgets/t/bush-calls-universal-broadband/#.Xec51JNKi_t.

BusinessDictionary.com. "Free Trade Agreement." n.d. Last modified December 3, 2019. www.businessdictionary.com/definition/free-trade-agreement.html.

Cartwright, Mark. "Piraeus." *Ancient History Encyclopedia*. 2013. Last modified December 3, 2019. www.ancient.eu/Piraeus/.

Cartwright, Mark. "Sui Dynasty." *Ancient History Encyclopedia*. 2017. Last modified December 3, 2019. www.ancient.eu/Sui_Dynasty/.

Chaudhury, Dipanjan Roy. "Africa Cancels a Belt and Road Initiative Project for the First Time." *The Economic Times*. Last modified October 25, 2018. https://economictimes.indiatimes.com/news/international/world-news/africa-cancels-a-bri-project-for-the-first-time/articleshow/66363312.cms.

Cheng, Evelyn. "Trade Tensions Have Had a 'Significant' Impact on China, IMF Says." *CNBC*. Last modified June 5, 2019. www.cnbc.com/2019/06/05/trade-tensions-have-had-a-significant-impact-on-china-imf-says.html.

"China and Maritime Nations, Sea Captains, Merchants, Merchandise, Passengers. 1800–1899." *The Maritime Heritage Projects: Ships, Captains, Merchants, Passengers to 1800s San Francisco*. Last modified December 3, 2019. https://maritimeheritage.org/ports/china.html.

"China COSCO Shipping COSCO SHIPPING Charity Foundation." *China COSCO Shipping*. Last modified December 3, 2019. http://en.coscocs.com/col/col6943/index.html.

China FTA Network. n.d. http://fta.mofcom.gov.cn/english/index.shtml.

"China, Greece Agree to Push Ahead with COSCO's Piraeus Port Investment." *Reuters*. Last modified November 11, 2019. www.reuters.com/article/us-greece-china/china-greece-agree-to-push-ahead-with-coscos-piraeus-port-investment-idUSKBN1XL1KC.

"China-Greece Relations in 'Best' Period since Diplomatic Ties Forged: President Hu." *The State Council The People's Republic of China*. n.d. www.gov.cn/misc/2006-01/20/content_166056.htm.

"China Profile." *BBC News.* Last modified July 29, 2019. www.bbc.com/news/world-asia-pacific-13017882.

China–Trade Agreements. 2019. www.export.gov/article?id=China-Trade-Agreements.

"China's Belt and Road Initiative in Latin America and the Caribbean." *IISS.* Last modified December 2018. www.iiss.org/publications/strategic-comments/2018/chinas-bri-in-latin-america.

"China's Economy Overtakes Japan." *BBC News.* Last modified February 14, 2011. www.bbc.com/news/business-12427321.

"Chios to Izmir." *Distance between Cities Places on Map Distance Calculator.* Last modified December 6, 2019. www.distancefromto.net/.

Chrepa, Eleni, and Slav Okov. "Bloomberg." *Bloomberg: Are You a Robot?* Last modified February 15, 2019. www.bloomberg.com/news/articles/2019-01-31/resolving-the-bitter-battle-over-the-name-macedonia-quicktake.

"Chronology." *Piraeus Port Authority S.A.* Last modified December 6, 2019. www.olp.gr/en/the-port-of-piraeus/chronology.

Congressional Research Service. "China's Economic Rise: History, Trends, Challenges, and Implications for the United States." *Federation of American Scientists: Science for a Safer, More Informed World.* Last modified June 25, 2019. https://fas.org/sgp/crs/row/RL33534.pdf.

"COSCO Global." *COSCO.* Last modified December 3, 2019. www.coscoshipping.gr/cosco-global/.

"COSCO Shipping Ports Buys Stake in Peruvian Chancay Terminal." *World Maritime News.* Last modified January 25, 2019. https://worldmaritimenews.com/archives/269604/cosco-shipping-ports-buys-stake-in-peruvian-chancay-terminal/.

"Costas Karamanlis Pictures and Photos." *Royalty Free Stock Photos, Illustrations, Vector Art and Video Clips: Getty Images.* Last modified December 6, 2019. www.gettyimages.ca/photos/costas-karamanlis?family=editorial&page=13&sort=best&phrase=costas%20karamanlis.

Cronin, Patrick M. "US-China Trade Deal: What It Is, Is Not, and May Become." *TheHill.* Last modified October 12, 2019. https://thehill.com/opinion/finance/465546-us-china-trade-deal-what-it-is-is-not-and-may-become.

Daily, China. "Belt and Road: Past, Present and Future." *The Telegraph.* Last modified May 2, 2019. www.telegraph.co.uk/china-watch/business/belt-road-projects-list/.

Definitions.net. "What Does Huaxia Mean?" n.d. Last modified December 3, 2019. www.definitions.net/definition/Huaxia.

"Dekemvriana, One of the Saddest Days in Greece's History." *Greek City Times.* Last modified December 3, 2019. https://greekcitytimes.com/2018/12/03/commemorating-dekemvriana-when-first-shots-are-fired-in-athens/.

Delloitte Group. "How Will CPEC Boost Pakistan Economy?" Last modified December 3, 2019. https://www2.deloitte.com/content/dam/Deloitte/pk/Documents/risk/pak-china-eco-corridor-deloittepk-noexp.pdf.

Deutsche Telekom AG. "Deutsche Telekom Raises Stake in OTE's Share Capital by 5 Percent." *Deutsche Telekom.* Last modified May 30, 2018. www.telekom.com/en/media/media-information/archive/deutsche-telekom-raises-stake-in-ote-s-share-capital-by-5-percent-526212.

Devonshire-Ellis, Chris. "China's Belt & Road Initiative and South America." *Silk Road Briefing.* Last modified May 29, 2019. www.silkroadbriefing.com/news/2019/05/29/chinas-belt-road-initiative-south-america/.

Dimas, Christos. "Privatization in the Name of 'Europe': Analyzing the Telecoms Privatization in Greece from a 'Discursive Institutionalist' Perspective." *LSE Research Online*. Last modified November 2010. http://eprints.lse.ac.uk/31089/1/GreeSE_No41.pdf.

"Disaster in Piraeus Harbour." *World War II Today*. Last modified December 3, 2019. http://ww2today.com/7th-april-1941-disaster-in-piraeus-harbour.

"Djibouti Signs Preliminary Deal with China's POLY-GCL for $4 Bln Gas Project." *Reuters*. Last modified November 16, 2017. www.reuters.com/article/china-djibouti-gas/djibouti-signs-preliminary-deal-with-chinas-poly-gcl-for-4-bln-gas-project-idUSL8N1NM2BV.

Dong, Carolyn, Matthew Davis, and Simin Yu. "China's One Belt One Road: Opportunities in Africa | | Insights | DLA Piper Global Law Firm." *DLA Piper*. Last modified November 5, 2018. www.dlapiper.com/en/southafrica/insights/publications/2018/11/africa-connected-doing-business-in-africa/chinas-one-belt-one-road-opportunities-in-africa/.

Dreyer, June Teufel. "The Belt, the Road, and Latin America." *Foreign Policy Research Institute*. Last modified January 16, 2019. www.fpri.org/article/2019/01/the-belt-the-road-and-latin-america/.

Duke University. "China's One Belt, One Road Plan Carries Environmental Risks." *Futurity*. Last modified May 10, 2019. www.futurity.org/one-belt-one-road-china-environmental-impact-2058742/.

"East China Sea Gas Field in Full Output: CNOOC." *The Japan Times*. Last modified August 5, 2006. www.japantimes.co.jp/news/2006/08/05/national/east-china-sea-gas-field-in-full-output-cnooc/#.Xecxf5NKi_t.

Ebrahimi, Helia. "The Big Fat Greek Sell-Off." *Telegraph.co.uk*. Last modified June 5, 2011. www.telegraph.co.uk/finance/financialcrisis/8556698/The-big-fat-Greek-sell-off.html.

The Economist. "The Third Industrial Revolution." 2012. Last modified December 3, 2019. www.economist.com/leaders/2012/04/21/the-third-industrial-revolution.

Economy Team. "Open Borders vs. Closed Borders: Economy." *Economy*. Last modified October 19, 2018. www.ecnmy.org/engage/open-borders-vs-closed-borders-which-is-better-for-the-economy/.

Editors, History.com. "China's Expansive History: Timeline." *HISTORY*. A&E Television Networks. 2019. Last modified December 3, 2019. www.history.com/topics/china/china-timeline.

Editors, History.com. "Industrial Revolution." *HISTORY*. A&E Television Network. 2019. Last modified December 3, 2019. www.history.com/topics/industrial-revolution/industrial-revolution.

Edwards, Jim. "500 Years Ago, China Destroyed Its World-Dominating Navy Because Its Political Elite Was Afraid of Free Trade." *Business Insider*. Last modified February 26, 2017. www.businessinsider.com/china-zhenge-he-treasure-fleet-elite-free-trade-2017-2.

"The Egnatia Motorway Vertical Axes and Their Significance." *Egnatia Motorway S.A.* Last modified December 3, 2019. www.egnatia.eu/page/default.asp?la=2&id=30.

"'Egnatia Railway." *European Commission | Choose Your Language | Choisir Une Langue | Wählen Sie Eine Sprache*. Last modified December 3, 2019. https://ec.europa.eu/eipp/desktop/en/projects/project-64.html.

Egnatia Railway. "Hellenic Republic Ministry of Infrastructure, Transport & Networks." n.d. www.ergose.gr/wp-content/uploads/2018/04/Sidirodromiki_Egnatia.pdf.

"Elucidate the Meaning of Ecological Sensitive Area (ESA) and Eco-Sensitive Zones (ESZs) While Bringing Out the Objectives of Their Demarcation." *GKToday*. Last modified

June 27, 2019. www.gktoday.in/answers/elucidate-the-meaning-of-ecological-sensitive-area-esa-and-eco-sensitive-zones-eszs-while-bringing-out-the-objectives-of-their-demarcation/.

Encyclopedia Britannica. "Crimean War." n.d. Last modified December 3, 2019. www.britannica.com/event/Crimean-War.

Encyclopedia Britannica. "Konstantinos Simitis." n.d. Last modified December 3, 2019. www.britannica.com/biography/Konstantinos-Simitis.

Encyclopedia Britannica. "Marco Polo." n.d. Last modified December 4, 2019. www.britannica.com/biography/Marco-Polo.

Encyclopædia Iranica. "ISIDORUS OF CHARAX: Encyclopaedia Iranica." 2012. Last modified December 3, 2019. www.iranicaonline.org/articles/isidorus-of-charax.

European Environment Information and Observation Network: Eionet Portal. "Ecologically Sensitive Area." General Multilingual Environmental Thesaurus. n.d. Last modified December 3, 2019. www.eionet.europa.eu/gemet/en/concept/2461.

European Stability Initiative. "Macedonia's Dispute with Greece: Macedonia." *European Stability Initiative: ESI*. Last modified November 2012. www.esiweb.org/index.php?lang=en&id=562.

"Exploration by Land: Silk and Spice Route Series." *UNESCO | Building Peace in the Minds of Men and Women*. Last modified 1993. https://en.unesco.org/silkroad/sites/silkroad/files/knowledge-bank-article/the%20end%20of%20the%20silk%20route.pdf.

Fabienkhan. "Persian Royal Road." *Ancient History Encyclopedia*. 2016. Last modified December 3, 2019. www.ancient.eu/image/5515/persian-royal-road/.

"Fig. 1. Aerial View of the Main (Passenger) Port of Piraeus." *ResearchGate*. Last modified March 1, 2018. www.researchgate.net/figure/Aerial-view-of-the-main-passenger-port-of-Piraeus_fig1_223548115.

Foreign Relations of the United States: Diplomatic Papers, 1945, the Near East and Africa, Volume VIII. Office of the Historian, Foreign Service Institute United States Department of State. 1945. https://history.state.gov/historicaldocuments/frus1945v08/d63.

FORUM ON CHINA-AFRICA COOPERATION BEIJING ACTION PLAN (2007–2009). Ministry of Foreign Affairs, the People's Republic of China. n.d. www.fmprc.gov.cn/zflt/eng/zyzl/hywj/t280369.htm.

"Four Modernizations." *Deng Xiaoping*. Last modified December 3, 2019. https://dengxiaopingproject.weebly.com/four-modernizations.html.

"Fourth Industrial Revolution." *World Economic Forum*. Last modified December 3, 2019. www.weforum.org/focus/fourth-industrial-revolution.

Frankopan, Peter. *The Silk Roads: A New History of the World*. New York: Vintage, 2016.

"Gansu Province." *Chinafolio*. n.d. www.chinafolio.com/provinces/gansu-province/.

Georgiopoulos, George. "China's Cosco Acquires 51 Pct Stake in Greece's Piraeus Port." *Reuters*. Last modified August 10, 2016. www.reuters.com/article/greece-privatisation-port/chinas-cosco-acquires-51-pct-stake-in-greeces-piraeus-port-idUSL8N1AR252.

"Global Growth Tracker." *World Economics: The Global Authority on Economic Data*. Last modified December 4, 2019. www.worldeconomics.com/%20papers/Global%20Growth%20Monitor_7c66ffca-ff86-4e4c-979d-7c5d7a22ef21.paper.

Globalization Monitor. "What Does 'China's One Belt, One Road' Might Means for the Environment?" *Intercoll*. Last modified February 11, 2019. https://intercoll.net/What-does-China-s-One-Belt-One-Road-might-means-for-the-environment.

Gontika, Tatiana. *Defining Maritime Cyber Terrorism*. Bronx, NY: SUNY Maritime College. 2019. Paper submitted as a term paper in TMGT 8499 Maritime Physical, Operational & Cyber Security.

Gonzalez, Joaquin V. "Argentine Cargo Rail Network Witnesses Great Improvements with China's Help–World–Chinadaily.com.cn." *Global Edition.* Last modified January 18, 2019. www.chinadaily.com.cn/a/201901/18/WS5c419473a3106c65c34e54d7.html.

"Great Stone Industrial Park." *Китайско-Белорусский индустриальный парк Великий камень—Главная.* Last modified December 3, 2019. https://industrialpark.by/en/about/general-information.html.

"Great Wall of China." *HISTORY.* A&E Television Networks. 2010. Last modified December 3, 2019. www.history.com/topics/ancient-china/great-wall-of-china.

"Greek Shipowners Agree to Pay 75 Million Euros Annually to State." *Reuters.* Last modified February 27, 2019. www.reuters.com/article/greece-shipping-taxation/greek-shipowners-agree-to-pay-75-million-euros-annually-to-state-idUSL5N20M60E.

"Greek Shipping and Economy 2019: The Strategic and Economic Role of Greek Shipping." *Hellenic Shipping News Worldwide,* Online Daily Newspaper on Hellenic and International Shipping. Last modified August 6, 2019. www.hellenicshippingnews.com/greek-shipping-and-economy-2019-the-strategic-and-economic-role-of-greek-shipping/.

Gupta, Anubhav. "Pakistan Confirms the Bugs in the Architecture of China's 'Belt and Road'." *World Politics Review | Analysis of International Affairs and Global Trends.* Last modified September 27, 2018. www.worldpoliticsreview.com/articles/26123/pakistan-confirms-the-bugs-in-the-architecture-of-china-s-belt-and-road.

Hadjimanolakis, Yannis E. "The Port of Piraeus Through the Ages." *Home: Hellenic Electronic Center.* Last modified December 3, 2019. www.greece.org/poseidon/work/sea-ports/piraeus.html.

Harlaftis, Gelina. *A History of Greek-Owned Shipping: The Making of an International Tramp Fleet, 1830 to the Present Day.* London: Routledge, 1995.

"HHI Builds Korea's First 10,000teu Containership." *Seatrade Maritime.* Last modified July 27, 2007. www.seatrade-maritime.com/asia/hhi-builds-koreas-first-10000teu-containership.

Hirst, Tomas. "A Brief History of China's Economic Growth." *World Economic Forum.* Last modified July 30, 2015. www.weforum.org/agenda/2015/07/brief-history-of-china-economic-growth/.

"The History of the Egnatia Motorway." *Egnatia Motorway S.A.* Last modified December 3, 2019. www.egnatia.eu/page/default.asp?la=2&id=23.

Howard, Lawrence A. "Geographic, Economic, Cultural, and Historical Contexts of Transportation Development." Lecture, Transportation Management–TMGT 73001, SUNY Maritime, New York, September 20, 2019.

"International Maritime Bureau." *ICC–Commercial Crime Services.* Last modified July 7, 2017. www.icc-ccs.org/icc/imb.

"Jammu and Kashmir." *Jammu and Kashmir.* Last modified December 8, 2019. www.google.com/maps/place/Jammu+and+Kashmir/@33.0469992,73.4518625,6.35z/data=!4m5!3m4!1s0x38e1092499ffa89d:0x6567a6d4697e7f1!8m2!3d33.778175!4d76.5761714.

Jennings, Ralph. "Japan Is Committing to China's Belt & Road Initiative, But What's in It for Them?" *Forbes.* Last modified April 17, 2018. www.forbes.com/sites/ralphjennings/2018/04/17/why-japan-had-to-join-china-in-building-trade-routes-around-asia/#18a59fa47175.

Kakissis, Joanna. "Chinese Firms Now Hold Stakes in over a Dozen European Ports." *NPR.org.* Last modified October 9, 2018. www.npr.org/2018/10/09/642587456/chinese-firms-now-hold-stakes-in-over-a-dozen-european-ports.

Kitsantonis, Niki. "Greece, 10 Years into Economic Crisis, Counts the Cost to Mental Health." *The New York Times: Breaking News, World News & Multimedia*. Last modified February 3, 2019. www.nytimes.com/2019/02/03/world/europe/greece-economy-mental-health.html.

Knowler, Greg. "China to Dominate Global Shipping by 2030, Shanghai Report Finds." *JOC. com | Container Shipping and Trade News and Analysis*. Last modified June 10, 2015. www.joc.com/maritime-news/china-dominate-global-shipping-2030-shanghai-report-finds_20150610.html.

Konstandaras, Nikos. "Opinion | Who Is Playing Politics with the Port of Piraeus?" *The New York Times: Breaking News, World News & Multimedia*. Last modified May 23, 2019. www.nytimes.com/2019/05/23/opinion/piraeus-greece-china.html.

Lagerwey, John. "Volume I." In *Religion and Chinese Society: Ancient and Medieval China*. Hong Kong: Chinese University Press, 2004.

Lam, Yin, and Karuna Ramakrishnan. "Three Factors That Have Made Singapore a Global Logistics Hub." *World Bank Blogs*. Last modified January 26, 2017. https://blogs.worldbank.org/transport/three-factors-have-made-singapore-global-logistics-hub.

Lau, Stuart. "Greece Gives Cosco Green Light for Partial Piraeus Port Upgrade." *South China Morning Post*. Last modified October 11, 2019. www.scmp.com/news/china/diplomacy/article/3032618/amid-headwinds-greece-gives-cosco-green-light-partial-piraeus.

Lee, Tae-Woo, Michael Roe, Richard Gray, and Mingnan Shen. *Shipping in China*. Aldershot: Gower Publishing, 2002. Reading.

Lee, Yen Nee. "US and China Could Sign 'Phase One' Trade Deal before Christmas, Pimco Predicts." *CNBC*. Last modified November 19, 2019. www.cnbc.com/2019/11/19/us-china-could-sign-phase-one-trade-deal-before-christmas-pimco-says.html.

Liu, Xinru. *The Silk Roads: A Brief History with Documents*. New York: Macmillan Higher Education, 2012.

Lowen, Mark. "Greek Debt Crisis: What Was the Point of the Referendum." *BBC News*. Last modified July 11, 2015. www.bbc.com/news/world-europe-33492387.

"Macedonia and Greece: Vote Settles 27-Year Name Dispute." *BBC News*. Last modified January 25, 2019. www.bbc.com/news/world-europe-47002865.

"The Macedonian Flag: Everything You Need to Know." *Discovering Macedonia*. Last modified March 25, 2019. www.discoveringmacedonia.com/2018/macedonian-flag-everything-need-know/.

"'Macedonia': Why Is a Name So Important?" *Political Geography Now*. Last modified September 28, 2018. www.polgeonow.com/2018/09/why-macedonia-is-so-important-greece-dispute.html.

Marcianus. *Périple de Marcien d'Héraclée, Epitome d'Artémidore, Isidore de Charax, etc. ou supplément aux dernières éditions des petits géographes* . . . 1839.

"Marco Polo and His Travels." *Silk Road*. Last modified December 3, 2019. www.silk-road.com/artl/marcopolo.shtml.

Maritimeatgreenwich. "Greek Shipping 1945–2010: A Success Story of Tradition, Innovation, Modernisation." *Maritime at Greenwich*. Last modified October 21, 2013. https://maritimeatgreenwich.wordpress.com/2013/10/21/greek-shipping-1945-2010-a-success-story-of-tradition-innovation-modernisation/.

The Maritime Executive. "Ocean Alliance Unveils Day 3 Product." *The Maritime Executive*. Last modified January 16, 2019. www.maritime-executive.com/article/ocean-alliance-unveils-day-3-product.

The Maritime Executive. "Top 10 Shipowning Nations: China Sees Biggest Increase." *The Maritime Executive*. Last modified February 6, 2019. www.maritime-executive.com/article/top-10-shipowning-nations-china-sees-biggest-increase.

McCurry, Justin. "China Overtakes Japan as World's Second-Largest Economy." *The Guardian*. Last modified November 26, 2017. www.theguardian.com/business/2011/feb/14/china-second-largest-economy.

McKenna, Amy. "Qing Dynasty." In *Encyclopedia Britannica*. 2019. Last modified December 3, 2019. www.britannica.com/topic/Qing-dynasty.

Mehta, Simi. "The Free and Open Indo-Pacific Strategy: A Way Forward." *Policy Forum*. Last modified July 25, 2019. www.policyforum.net/the-free-and-open-indo-pacific-strategy-a-way-forward/.

Meunier, Sophie. "A Tale of Two Ports: The Epic Story of Chinese Direct Investment in the Greek Port of Piraeus." *CritCom | A Forum for Research and Commentary on Europe*. Last modified December 14, 2015. http://critcom.councilforeuropeanstudies.org/a-tale-of-two-ports-the-epic-story-of-chinese-direct-investment-in-the-greek-port-of-piraeus/.

"Milestones." *COSCO SHIPPING*. Last modified December 4, 2019. www.coscointl.com/en/about-us/cosco-shipping-international/about-milestones/.

The Military Junta in Greece (1967–1974). Let's meet in Thessaloniki, July 23, 2018. Last modified December 3, 2019. www.meetinthessaloniki.eu/en/the-military-junta-in-greece-1967-1974/.

MI News Network. "10 Largest Container Shipping Companies in the World." *Marine Insight*. Last modified October 20, 2019. www.marineinsight.com/know-more/10-largest-container-shipping-companies-in-the-world/.

Ming, Cheang. "'Best Time in History' for China-Russia Relationship: Xi and Putin Boost Ties." *CNBC*. Last modified July 5, 2017. www.cnbc.com/2017/07/04/china-russia-ties-reaffirmed-after-xi-jinping-and-vladimir-putin-meet.html.

Miyake, Kuni. "What Does the 'Indo-Pacific Strategy' Mean?" *The Japan Times*. Last modified March 11, 2019. www.japantimes.co.jp/opinion/2019/03/11/commentary/japan-commentary/indo-pacific-strategy-mean/#.Xec4qJNKi_t.

Nachmani, Amikam. *March 2016: The Greek Civil War, 1946–1949 | Origins: Current Events in Historical Perspective*. Origins: Current Events in Historical Perspective. 2016. https://origins.osu.edu/milestones/march-2016-greek-civil-war-1946-1949.

Naughton, Barry, Arthur R. Kroeber, Guy De Jonquierres, and Graham Webster. "What Will the TPP Mean for China?" *Foreign Policy*. Last modified October 7, 2015. https://foreignpolicy.com/2015/10/07/china-tpp-trans-pacific-partnership-obama-us-trade-xi/.

Nayyar, Sarita, and Zara Ingilizian. "Future of Consumption in Fast-Growth Consumer Markets: China." *World Economic Forum: Home*. Last modified January 2018. http://www3.weforum.org/docs/WEF_Future_of_Consumption_in_Fast_Growth_Consumer_Markets_China.pdf.

NDR. "Aristoteles Onassis: Mit Tankern an Die Spitze." *NDR.de–Das Beste Am Norden–Radio–Fernsehen–Nachrichten | NDR.de*. Last modified December 6, 2019. www.ndr.de/geschichte/chronologie/Aristoteles-Onassis-Mit-Tankern-an-die-Spitze,onassis106.html.

"Network." *Welcome: EcoPorts | ESPO*. Last modified December 3, 2019. www.ecoports.com/network.

"Newly Formed Ocean Alliance Has Huge Impact on Container Shipping." *Your Global Logistics Network*. Last modified December 3, 2019. https://atlas-network.com/newly-formed-ocean-alliance-has-huge-impact-on-container-shipping/.

Niiler, Eric. "How the Second Industrial Revolution Changed Americans' Lives." *HISTORY*. 2019. Last modified December 3, 2019. www.history.com/news/second-industrial-revolution-advances.

"Ocean Alliance: The World's Largest Operational Agreement between Shipping Companies Is Extended until 2027." *CMA CGM*. Last modified January 18, 2019. www.cma-cgm.com/news/2379/ocean-alliance-the-world-s-largest-operational-agreement-between-shipping-companies-is-extended-until-2027.

"One Belt One Road Initiative, the Belt and Road Map & List & Impact." *Top China Travel Agency, Top China Tours, China Travel Service*. Last modified December 3, 2019. www.topchinatravel.com/silk-road/one-belt-one-road.htm.

"PERS." *Welcome: EcoPorts | ESPO*. Last modified December 3, 2019. www.ecoports.com/pers.

Petropoulos, Sotiris. "Greek Shipping Industry, One Belt, One Road (OBOR) and the Greek: Chinese Relations." Presentation, Athens, March 30, 2016.

Pham, Peter. "Why Did Donald Trump Kill This Big Free Trade Deal?" *Forbes*. Last modified December 29, 2017. www.forbes.com/sites/peterpham/2017/12/29/why-did-donald-trump-kill-this-big-free-trade-deal/#3dca15fb4e62.

Piccirilli Dorsey, Inc. "Exploring the Environmental Repercussions of China's Belt and Road Initiative." *Environmental and Energy Study Institute | Ideas: Insights: Sustainable Solutions*. Last modified October 30, 2018. www.eesi.org/articles/view/exploring-the-environmental-repercussions-of-chinas-belt-and-road-initiativ.

"Piraeus." *The Maritime Heritage Projects: Ships, Captains, Merchants, Passengers to 1800s San Francisco*. Last modified 2017. www.maritimeheritage.org/ports/greecePiraeus.

Plafker, Ted. "A Year Later, China's Stimulus Package Bears Fruit." *The New York Times: Breaking News, World News & Multimedia*. Last modified October 22, 2009. www.nytimes.com/2009/10/23/business/global/23iht-rglobalchin.html.

Pletcher, Kenneth. "Bamboo Annals." In *Encyclopedia Britannica*. n.d. Last modified December 3, 2019. www.britannica.com/topic/Bamboo-Annals.

Polo, Marco. *Le Livre des merveilles du monde*. Paris: J'ai Lu, 2017.

Poskus, Nerijus. "Guide to Ocean Alliances." *Flexport: Digital Freight Forwarder & Customs Broker*. Last modified December 11, 2015. www.flexport.com/blog/what-are-ocean-alliances.

Premier Wen Jiabao Meets with Greek Prime Minister George Papandreou. Embassy of the People's Republic of China in the United States of America. 2010. www.china-embassy.org/eng/zgyw/t759474.htm.

"Premier Wen Makes Five-Point Proposal on China-Greece Ties." *Xinhua English*. Last modified October 2, 2010. http://english.sina.com/china/p/2010/1002/342089.html.

Rajagopalan, Rajeswari Pillai. "Are China-India Relations Really Improving?" *The Diplomat*. Last modified March 1, 2018. https://thediplomat.com/2018/03/are-china-india-relations-really-improving/.

Ramasamy, Bala. "Why China Could Never Sign on to the Trans-Pacific Partnership." *The Conversation*. Last modified April 13, 2016. https://theconversation.com/why-china-could-never-sign-on-to-the-trans-pacific-partnership-56361.

Ramburuth, Prem, Christina Stringer, and Manuel Serapio. *Dynamics of International Business: Asia-Pacific Business Cases*. Cambridge: Cambridge University Press, 2013.

Rankin, Jennifer. "Greece in Europe: A Short History." *The Guardian*. Last modified July 3, 2015. www.theguardian.com/world/2015/jul/03/greece-in-europe-a-short-history.

Ray, Michael. "George Papandreou." In *Encyclopedia Britannica*. n.d. Last modified December 3, 2019. www.britannica.com/biography/George-Papandreou.

Ray, Michael. "Kostas Karamanlis." In *Encyclopedia Britannica*. n.d. Last modified December 3, 2019. www.britannica.com/biography/Kostas-Karamanlis.

RFE/RL's Turkmen Service. "Uzbek, Turkmen Presidents Agree to Cooperation on Energy, Transportation, Security." *Radio Free Europe/Radio Liberty*. Last modified March 6, 2017. www.rferl.org/a/uzbekistan-turkmenistan-mirziyaev-berdymukhammedov/28354163.html.

Rivlin, Helen Anne B. "Mu'ammad 'Al | Pasha and Viceroy of Egypt." In *Encyclopedia Britannica*. n.d. Last modified December 3, 2019. www.britannica.com/biography/Muhammad-Ali-pasha-and-viceroy-of-Egypt.

Rohn, Peter H. *Treaty Profiles*. Santa Barbara, CA: Clio Books, 1976.

Rosenberg, Matt. "The Major Sectors of the Economy." *ThoughtCo*. Last modified May 6, 2019. www.thoughtco.com/sectors-of-the-economy-1435795.

Salikha, Adelaida. "World's Top 10 Ship Owning Nations 2019 | Seasia.co." *Good News from Southeast Asia*. Last modified February 8, 2019. https://seasia.co/2019/02/08/world-s-top-10-ship-owning-nations-2019.

Schottenhammer, Angela. "The 'China Seas' in World History: A General Outline of the Role of Chinese and East Asian Maritime Space from Its Origins to C. 1800." *ScienceDirect. com | Science, Health and Medical Journals, Full Text Articles and Books*. Last modified December 2012. www.sciencedirect.com/science/article/pii/S2212682112000261.

Schwab, Klaus. "The Fourth Industrial Revolution." *Foreign Affairs*. Last modified December 12, 2015. www.foreignaffairs.com/articles/2015-12-12/fourth-industrial-revolution.

Schwab, Klaus. "The Fourth Industrial Revolution: What It Means and How to Respond." *World Economic Forum*. Last modified January 14, 2016. www.weforum.org/agenda/2016/01/the-fourth-industrial-revolution-what-it-means-and-how-to-respond/.

"Second Belt and Road Forum Top-Level Attendees." *The Diplomat: The Diplomat Is a Current-Affairs Magazine for the Asia-Pacific, with News and Analysis on Politics, Security, Business, Technology and Life across the Region*. Last modified April 27, 2019. https://thediplomat.com/2019/04/second-belt-and-road-forum-top-level-attendees/.

Senate of the United States of America, U. S.–China Security Review Commission, and U. S. Government. *China's Belt and Road Initiative (BRI): Five Years Later: Economic, Military, Geostrategic Drivers and Implications, Regional Reactions, Xi Jinping's Vision, Pakistan, Nepal, Bangladesh Difficulties*. 2019.

Shams, Shamil. "Belt and Road Forum: Is the China-Pakistan Economic Corridor Failing?" *DW.COM*. Last modified April 25, 2017. www.dw.com/en/belt-and-road-forum-is-the-china-pakistan-economic-corridor-failing/a-48473486.

"Shareholder Agreement Renewed between COSCO SHIPPING International Hong Kong and Jotun A/S." *COSCO SHIPPING*. Last modified December 4, 2019. www.coscointl.com/en/media-centre/news-release/shareholder-agreement-renewed-between-cosco-shipping-international-hong-kong-and-jotun-as/.

Sikdar, Chandrima, and Kakali Mukhopadhyay. "Economy-Wide Impact of TPP: New Challenges to China." *Journal of Economic Structures*. Last modified September 13, 2017. https://journalofeconomicstructures.springeropen.com/articles/10.1186/s40008-017-0082-y.

Smith, Helena. "Chinese Carrier Cosco Is Transforming Piraeus and Has Eyes on Thessaloniki." *The Guardian*. Last modified June 19, 2014. www.theguardian.com/world/2014/jun/19/china-piraeus-greece-cosco-thessaloniki-railways.

Smith, Helena. "Xi Jinping Comes to Greeks Bearings Gifts." *The Guardian*. Last modified November 12, 2019. www.theguardian.com/world/2019/nov/12/xi-jinping-comes-to-greeks-bearings-gifts.

Smith, Rob. "The World's Biggest Economies in 2018." *World Economic Forum*. Last modified April 18, 2018. www.weforum.org/agenda/2018/04/the-worlds-biggest-economies-in-2018/.

Snow, Shawn. "Analysis: Why Kashmir Matters." *The Diplomat: The Diplomat is a Current-Affairs Magazine for the Asia-Pacific, with News and Analysis on Politics, Security, Business, Technology and Life across the Region*. Last modified September 20, 2016. https://thediplomat.com/2016/09/analysis-why-kashmir-matters/.

Sparks, Karen. "Giorgios Papadopoulos." In *Encyclopedia Britannica*. n.d. Last modified December 3, 2019. www.britannica.com/biography/Giorgios-Papadopoulos.

Sustainable Ports in the Adriatic-Ionian Region. European Union. 2018. https://supair.adrioninterreg.eu/.

Swanson, Ana. "Trump Reaches 'Phase 1' Deal with China and Delays Planned Tariffs." *The New York Times: Breaking News, World News & Multimedia*. Last modified November 12, 2019. www.nytimes.com/2019/10/11/business/economy/us-china-trade-deal.html.

Syrrakos, Dimitrios. "China's Relationships with Greece and Italy Are Deepening: EU Is Reaping Exactly What It Sowed." *The Conversation*. Last modified November 18, 2019. https://theconversation.com/chinas-relationships-with-greece-and-italy-are-deepening-eu-is-reaping-exactly-what-it-sowed-127087?fbclid=IwAR2DQA6ZF9pq9UQE1v8_yzo4SbSgM5kqN1OOLyK_NzoUGvesE_c_jTsPEyw.

Tafero, Arthur. *The Belt and Road Research Text Book: 2nd Edition Br 001: Understanding the Belt and Road*. Scotts Valley: Createspace Independent Publishing Platform, 2018.

Tafero, Paul E., and Arthur H. Tafero. *China Strategies in the Belt and Road Initiative*. Independently Published, 2019. https://www.bookdepository.com/China-Strategies-Belt-Road-Initiative-Paul-Eberle-Dr-Arthur-Tafero/9781095227565.

"Taiwan." *The Maritime Heritage Project*. Last modified December 3, 2019. www.maritimeheritage.org/ports/taiwan.html.

Taylor, Paul. "Syriza's Greek Victory a Mixed Blessing for European Left." *Reuters*. Last modified September 21, 2015. www.reuters.com/article/uk-eurozone-greece-election-left-idAFKCN0RL1TA20150921.

Theotokas, I., and G. Harlaftis. *Leadership in World Shipping: Greek Family Firms in International Business*. Basingstoke: Springer, 2009.

Thomas, Landon, Jr. "Greece's Debt-Ridden Rail System Adds to Economic Breakdown." *The New York Times: Breaking News, World News & Multimedia*. Last modified July 20, 2010. www.nytimes.com/2010/07/21/business/global/21rail.html.

Tikkanen, Amy. "Konstantinos Mitsotakis." In *Encyclopedia Britannica*. n.d. Last modified December 3, 2019. www.britannica.com/biography/Konstantinos-Mitsotakis.

Tikkanen, Amy. "Special Economic Zone." In *Encyclopedia Britannica*. n.d. Last modified December 3, 2019. www.britannica.com/topic/special-economic-zone.

"Timeline." *OTE*. Last modified December 3, 2019. www.cosmote.gr/cs/otegroup/en/otegroup_timeline.html.

Toppa, Sabrina. "Why Young Pakistanis Are Learning Chinese." *The Atlantic*. Last modified November 14, 2018. www.theatlantic.com/international/archive/2018/11/pakistan-china-cooperation-cpec/568750/.

"Trains in Greece." *RailPass.com | Eurail and Europe Rail Pass Experts*. Last modified December 3, 2019. www.railpass.com/trains/greece.

Tzannatos, Ernestos. "Fig. 1. Aerial View of the Main (Passenger) Port of Piraeus." *ResearchGate*. Last modified April 25, 2018. www.researchgate.net/figure/Aerial-view-of-the-main-passenger-port-of-Piraeus_fig1_223548115.

Tziampiris, Aristotle. "Greece, European Political Cooperation and the Macedonian Question June 1991–December 1992." PhD diss., London School of Economics. 1999. ProQuest.

Ullyett, Richard. "COSCO Signs Agreement with Another Mediterranean Port." *PortSEurope*. Last modified February 12, 2019. www.portseurope.com/cosco-signs-agreement-with-another-mediterranean-port/.

Ullyett, Richard. "Piraeus Port Authority Details Environmental Plan." *PortSEurope*. Last modified February 24, 2019. www.portseurope.com/piraeus-port-authority-details-environmental-plan/.

Vineyard, Jared. "Freight History: China and International Shipping." *Universal Cargo*. Last modified February 9, 2018. www.universalcargo.com/freight-history-china-and-international-shipping/.

Volanakis, Constantinos. "The Port of Piraeus." 1886. https://twitter.com/ArcGreek/status/1116961945532366848.

"Voters Don't Understand the Question." *The National Herald*. Last modified July 4, 2015. www.thenationalherald.com/90180/?utm_source=feedburner&utm_medium=feed&utm_campaign=Feed%3A+TNHTopStories+%28The+National+Herald+top+stories%29.

Walt, Vivienne. "Boxed In at the Docks: How a Lifeline from China Changed Greece." *Fortune*. Last modified July 22, 2019. https://fortune.com/longform/cosco-piraeus-port-athens/.

Wen, Yi. "China's Rise from Agrarian Society to Industrial Power in Just 35 Years." *Federal Reserve Bank of St. Louis | Economic Data, Monetary Rates, Economic Education*. Last modified April 12, 2016. www.stlouisfed.org/publications/regional-economist/april-2016/chinas-rapid-rise-from-backward-agrarian-society-to-industrial-powerhouse-in-just-35-years.

Wong, Peter. "A New Future for the World Economy." *HSBC Commercial Banking | HSBC*. Last modified June 14, 2018. www.business.hsbc.com/belt-and-road/a-new-future-for-the-world-economy.

World Maritime News Staff. "Construction Starts at Damerjog LNG Terminal in Djibouti." *World Maritime News*. Last modified March 3, 2016. https://worldmaritimenews.com/archives/184628/construction-starts-at-damerjog-lng-terminal-in-djibouti/.

Xiang, Wang. "Port Deal among 16 Sino-Greek Contracts Sealed." *SHINE*. Last modified November 12, 2019. www.shine.cn/news/nation/1911125888/.

Xiao, Cai. "China, Russia Set Up RMB Investment Fund." *Global Edition*. Last modified July 5, 2017. www.chinadaily.com.cn/business/2017-07/05/content_30002107.htm.

Xin, Zhang. "Indian Ambassador to China Optimistic about Future of Bilateral Relations." *Global Times*. Last modified January 25, 2018. www.globaltimes.cn/content/1086596.shtml.

Xing, Li. *Mapping China's 'One Belt One Road' Initiative*. London: Palgrave Macmillan, 2018.

Xiwen, Xu, and Michael W. Hansen. "The Arrival of Chinese Investors in Denmark a Survey of Recent Trends in Chinese FDI in Denmark." Copenhagen Business School. Last modified August 7, 2017. https://pdfs.semanticscholar.org/9341/a00906192ab5d7e815512b4d98b9d7a4b25a.pdf.

Yousafzai, Fawad. "Work on CASA-1000 Power Project in Full Swing: Tajik Diplomat." *The Nation*. Last modified July 19, 2018. https://nation.com.pk/19-Jul-2018/work-on-casa-1000-power-project-in-full-swing-tajik-diplomat.

Ιστορία. "Αθήνα: Κεντρικό Αρχαιολογικό Συμβούλιο & Συμβούλιο Μουσείων." 2015. http://kas.culture.gr/%ce%b9%cf%83%cf%84%ce%bf%cf%81%ce%af%ce%b1/.

Καψής, Μανόλης. "Με μία φράση η Μυρσίνη Ζορμπά τα είπε όλα . . . Οι επενδύσεις είναι αυθαίρετες." *Capital.gr.* Last modified April 6, 2019. www.capital.gr/arthra/3352998/me-mia-frasi-i-mursini-zormpa-ta-eipe-ola-oi-ependuseis-einai-authairetes.

Κύρωση Σύμβασης Παραχώρησης μεταξύ Ελληνικού Δημοσίου και της Οργανισμός Λιμένοσ Πειραιώς και άλλεσ διστάξεις. Hellenic Parliament. n.d. www.hellenicparliament.gr/UserFiles/bcc26661-143b-4f2d-8916-0e0e66ba4c50/p-limen-pap-sunolo.pdf.

Λουκέρη, Σοφία. *Κώστας Καραμανλής, Το Τελευταίο Εμπόδιο.* Αθήνα: Εκδόσεις Ιππόκαμπος, 2017.

Παπαστεφάνου, Βίκυ. "Μυρσίνη Ζορμπά: Χάρτινα Βέλη Οι Αντιδράσεις Εναντίον Του ΚΑΣ Για Τον Πειραιά." *Αθήνα 9.84.* Last modified April 4, 2019. http://athina984.gr/wp-site/2019/04/04/myrsini-zormpa-chartina-veli-oi-antidraseis-enantion-toy-kasgia-ton-peiraia/.

Σημίτης, Κώστας. "Η Μεταπολίτευση, μία σύντομη αποτίμηση." *Η Καθημερινή* (Αθήνα), July 20, 2014. www.kathimerini.gr/776962/opinion/epikairothta/politikh/h-metapoliteysh-mia-syntomh-apotimhsh.

Index

Page numbers in *italics* indicate a figure on the corresponding page.

Printed in the United States
by Baker & Taylor Publisher Services

Printed in the United States
by Baker & Taylor Publisher Services